AI

How the Church Has Changed the World

Volume IV

January 2020 – December 2021

MAGNIFICAT

Paris • New York • Oxford • Madrid

Publisher: Romain Lizé
Editor-in-Chief: Rev. Sebastian White, O.P.
Managing Editor: David Wharton
Iconography: Isabelle Mascaras
Layout: Julia Pateu
Cover: Diane Danis
Proofreading: Samuel Wigutow
Front cover: *Church of Eragny* (1886), Lucien Pissaro (1863-1944), Ashmolean Museum, Oxford, UK. © akg-images.

Printed in 2023 in France by Sepec – 11355221103
First edition: 2023
ISBN: 978-1-63967-051-2

CONTENTS

Sanctity
No Elder than a Boy

Many a lover of man's best friend has hoped to find a shaggy welcome in heaven, as if the old fellow would wag his tail to say, "It's you! I'm glad you made it. I wasn't sure." But what about a dog sent *from* heaven? A big gray scruffy wolf of a dog, who appears out of nowhere when you're in trouble, and when you look around after the thieves or killers have run away, he's gone? Saint John Bosco had that dog, or the dog had him. It's hard to tell which.

I'll tell about the dog because I'm telling about the boy that John Bosco was. There are two kinds of people who should never teach boys: people who don't like boys or know what they are, and people who do not like men or know what they are. John Bosco was the greatest teacher of boys the modern world has seen, and that was partly because he remained a boy all his life long.

More than one kind of beast

John Bosco was only a small boy when, one night, he dreamed he was being pursued by ferocious animals, but while he was running away, a woman's voice told him instead to bring those animals into pasture. So he did, and they became a flock of gentle sheep. John took the dream to heart, and when he grew up and became a parish priest in Turin, he saw plenty that was wild and fierce roaming the streets. They were the homeless boys of that big city, black with soot from the factories. Those boys were growing up to be worse than beasts. John Bosco's heart went out to them.

What would you do if you wanted to bring God to rough boys on the streets? Whatever you'd do, it would help if you had the physique for it. John Bosco had that strength. He grew up doing hard physical work on his mother's plot of land in the country, which she and he and his brother had to tend themselves after the father died—plowing, planting, reaping, caring for the cows and horses and pigs, and keeping the vineyard. But John also had a hobby that did not require shovels and pitchforks. He would set up a small stage in front of his friends and repeat what the priest had said on Sunday. So has many an altar boy done. But John added things that the priest couldn't have done without earning him a visit to the bishop. John walked on his hands and did cartwheels. He did magic tricks, picking coins out of people's ears. He did as a boy the things he would later do *for the boys.* He was already an athlete for God.

Let me have the boy

When he became a priest, John Bosco did not forget that he had been a boy. He could be found walking a tightrope in front of twenty cheering and very dirty boys, catching their attention by his strength and agility, and winning their hearts with his good humor and his love.

Who was the first boy that Father John Bosco—Don Bosco, as they called him—saved from poverty and ignorance? One day he overheard his sacristan scolding a teenage boy, a ragged lad from the streets. He wanted the boy to serve Mass, but they boy said he didn't know how to do it. "Then get lost!" hollered the sacristan, but Don Bosco interrupted.

"Let me have the boy," he said.

The boy's name was Bartolomeo Garelli. He was about sixteen. Did he know when to kneel at Mass and when to stand? He didn't even know how to make the sign of the cross. Don Bosco taught him how, and made him promise to return the next day. The boy kept his promise, won over by the priest's kindness. But he did more than keep his promise, just as Don Bosco was more than simply kind. Bartolomeo brought a couple of other boys with him. That is how Don Bosco's ministry to the wayside youth of Turin began. If the boy had a home, Don Bosco would visit him there, and meet his mother and father and his brothers and sisters. If the boy wanted food, he got it for him. All the boys, just like the rest of us, needed the grace of God, so he took them to Mass and instructed them in the faith. They needed recreation, so he took them also to the park, where he mingled instruction with games and athletic feats.

Kindness, not punishment

You must not think that Don Bosco was a man of ordinary intelligence who was simply good with children. He was a brilliant man. He wrote more books in his life than a lot of people have read—nearly a hundred. His superiors gave him the chance to be a professor at a university, and he would have taken it, because he was an obedient priest, but he told them that he still felt he needed to take care of the poor children—that was where his calling lay. Three hundred boys—and his ministry was just beginning!

Imagine having three hundred boys playing in the courtyard of your church. Not all priests were happy about that, or the parishioners either. Boys are noisy creatures. They trample the grass. The ball they're kicking bounces off into the flowerbeds. All kinds of terrible things like that can happen. So you must imagine Don Bosco leading the boys on a Sunday walk, miles and miles into the countryside, arriving at a church, asking permission to say Mass there, doing so with all those boys in attendance, then having breakfast in the open air, followed by play, and catechism, and the long walk back into Turin, singing hymns as a choir would sing them, and praying the rosary. The boys would remember those Sundays for the rest of their lives.

Don Bosco went on to found the Salesians, named after Saint Francis de Sales. The Salesians follow the wisdom of their founder. Kindness, not punishment, was the key; Don Bosco could always obtain from his boys the obedience he wanted by being kind to them, by praising their good works, and by showing them that he loved them and would do anything he could to feed them, house them, teach them, and build their souls. During the life of Don Bosco, the Salesians spread to several countries and ministered to hundreds of thousands of boys.

Our needs are just as great now as their need was then. How many boys in our time grow up without a father, to model for them, if only in a distant way, the love of the Father?

Mamma and the dog

But I will conclude with two more things that should warm the hearts of boys everywhere.

One was the mother. Many of the boys were orphans, and whether they were or not, Don Bosco was a man, and a boy needs a mother's care too, something he could not give them. That was why he begged his mother Margarita to come and join them. It meant a great sacrifice for her to leave her beloved little cottage in the country, and the farm she had worked from the time she was married, to go to dingy and noisy and dangerous Turin, the big city, and be mother, housemaid, nurse, and teacher to hundreds of boys. But she did it. They called her Mamma Margarita, and what that one old woman did freed Don Bosco to build more and more—teaching, always teaching, establishing the Oratory of Saint Francis, hiring professors for it, and reaping the reward of vocations to the priesthood. Man and woman, mother and son, working together as if in a dance, as God intended it to be.

The other was a dog named Grigio. He was three feet tall at the shoulder, as big as a Newfoundland or a mastiff. He had thick white-gray fur, and a muzzle like a wolf's. He could put the fear of dog into the criminals who infested the alleys of the city. Where did Don Bosco find him? Nowhere. Don Bosco did not find him. Grigio found Don Bosco. "It was not you who chose me," said Jesus to the apostles, "but I who chose you."

Often, when Don Bosco was walking from the country into Turin, or walking the city's streets at night, this magnificent animal appeared out of nowhere to walk beside him, just when assassins were about to waylay him. Once, Grigio pinned a thug by the throat, and would have killed him if the man hadn't pleaded with Don Bosco to call his dog off. The boys loved Grigio, but nobody ever gave him any food. Grigio refused, even when once they got him to enter the refectory where everybody took their meals. Grigio came and went when Don Bosco needed his protection, and that was that.

He even appeared to the priest and a friend of his thirty years later, when they were lost at night in a dangerous marsh. "If only my Grigio were here!" cried Don Bosco, when sure enough, there was the dog, who led them by a meandering path out of the danger.

The dog may have been a guardian angel. But wouldn't our own dogs be guardian angels, if they could?

Pilgrimage into Poverty

I'm writing this month about Lourdes, and my fingers should tremble. Six million people visit the grotto every year. I've never been there. Franz Werfel, a Jew, wrote a fine book about Saint Bernadette's visions, and how no one believed her at first, not even her family; how she was ridiculed, slapped in prison, called a fraud by skeptics; how she maintained her simple faith throughout; and her honest account of the facts.

The journalist Malcolm Muggeridge—he who would introduce the world to Mother Teresa in the 1969 documentary *Something Beautiful for God*—accompanied a pilgrimage to Lourdes with his film crew in 1965. This was long before he and his wife entered the Church in their very old age. He didn't witness what the Church, with her severe criteria, would certify as a miraculous cure. But he recalled the *beauty* of the place; the light shining in the eyes of a young lady, crippled and dying, whom he had met and spoken to as she went down to the waters. He believed, in a way he couldn't yet describe, that Jesus the healer was present: "At Lourdes, too, bowing their heads, abating their twitchings, holding out their hands, if they have any, as the Blessed Sacrament approaches, they recall his healing words: *Daughter, your faith has made you whole; go in peace.*"

There's no place in the world like Lourdes. To go there in faith is to make a pilgrimage into poverty. Muggeridge would understand, because he had seen through the vanity of what the world calls great. Mother Teresa would understand. Muslims go to Mecca, to adore the *power* of God. Hindus go to the mighty Ganges River to immerse themselves in the waters of an ancient mythology. But Lourdes? It's a mustard seed by comparison. It's a bit of leaven that an ordinary woman kneaded into some dough. It is a pearl hidden in a field. It is a stone that the builders tossed aside.

The girl was small

To whom should the Virgin Mother appear? To such as Bernadette Soubirous. Her family lived in terrible poverty. At the time the visions came, their rented home was an old jail cell, twelve feet square, with a stinking privy in the back. Bernadette was only beginning, at age fourteen, to learn to read. Lourdes was a forgotten village in the foothills of the Pyrenees. "Can anything good come from Nazareth?" asked Nathanael, but that was before he met Jesus.

On a cold and rainy day, February 11, 1858, Bernadette, her sister, and a friend went out gathering sticks for firewood. Think of Elijah and the widow and her son, in the years of famine. The grotto of Massabielle had no glorious spired basilica on it then. It was a muddy and miserable place, a watering hole for pigs, where the Gave River washed up all kinds of garbage, some of which the poor children would gather up and sell.

Bernadette wasn't there to play a game. The other girls had crossed the river, which was so cold it made them cry. Bernadette needed to get across too, so she asked the girls to toss some rocks into the water for stepping stones, while she was busy sitting down, taking off her stockings. That was all she was thinking of, the practical matter of getting across the river without bringing on an attack of her asthma or ruining the stockings.

Then she turned and saw a lady dressed in white, silently saying the rosary.

She didn't know who it was. She even told the girls to keep quiet about it. She didn't trust her judgment. That's why she brought holy water to the grotto the next time she felt drawn to visit it, to splash upon the lady, in case it was an evil spirit. But the lady smiled.

She told Bernadette to come to the grotto every day for a fortnight. We might say that the pilgrimages began then. Her family came with her. People in the village came. The police had to come to keep order. Curiosity seekers came. Scoffers and skeptics came. Christians came.

What did they come to see? On February 25, the lady made Bernadette smaller than ever: she told her to do two things that no one could understand. She was to go crawl underneath a projecting rock and drink from the "fountain" there; and to eat some of the grass. There was no fountain. It was a small puddle, more mud than water. Bernadette scratched at it until she could drink a little, and she ate the grass, too. Imagine her muddy face, flecked with weeds. Who could believe in her visions now? Even her family lost heart.

But the spring bubbled up beneath the mud. After the miraculous cure of a paralytic woman, the crowds returned, much to the chagrin of the local police. In all of this, Bernadette never put herself forward. All she did was to keep her promise to the lady, to return to the grotto, where she prayed silently, her countenance glowing with both sadness and joy.

The Immaculate Conception

Bernadette's parish priest, an impatient fellow, finally told the girl to demand from the lady her name. This came after the lady had commanded a sacred procession to the grotto, and a chapel to be built at the site. The procession was the first organized pilgrimage to Lourdes. Ten thousand people were there. But Bernadette still did not know the lady's name. She did not presume to know. She didn't even admit that she had been responsible for any cures. She refused all money. She wanted only to obey the lady, and to study for her First Communion.

The fortnight passed. The Soubirous family was as poor as ever. Lourdes was thronged with visitors. Bernadette had returned to her ordinary life. Then on March 25, she heard the call again, and this time the lady revealed her name, in the girl's dialect. Tell the priest, she said, *Que soy era Immaculada Councepciou:* "I am the Immaculate Conception."

Bernadette rehearsed the strange words on her way to the priest. She didn't know what they meant. Pope Pius IX had recently declared as a matter of faith that Mary had been conceived without taint of original sin. Bernadette did not know that. The priest did—and he was stunned.

How shall I put these things together? A young man with his hip devoured by cancer enters the waters of Lourdes. He has, on one side, *no hip at all.* When he returns from Lourdes, he begins again to walk and run as he used to do. X-rays show that there is no more sarcoma. Instead there is a hip, sound and sure.

Where did that come from? You can't persuade your body to make new tissue out of nothing. The new bone came from the smallest of places, that mustard seed, that leaven. What lies within the smallest of the seeds? God Almighty does: the power that made the universe from nothing, the eternity that is wholly present in every smallest twitch of an atom. It's no more difficult for God to make worlds than for him to make cells rush in multiplication and build up bone; each is as nothing at all, to God.

When the flesh of Mary began to be knit in the womb of her mother Anne, what then was the work of God? He wrought a miracle, preserving Mary from that fall of Adam that is the shadow that falls upon each of us when we are conceived. We are born paralytics, hunched toward sin and death. Mary was born in full health of soul. She stood upright.

Christ the healer

By 1908, the fiftieth anniversary of the apparition of Mary to little Bernadette, the Lourdes researcher Georges Bertrin had counted 3,962 bodily cures. Only about one in fourteen of these were of nervous conditions. Many of the rest involved the inexplicable and immediate growth of healthy tissue. Bertrin says also that even if some of the cures were doubtful, a far greater number of cures were never recorded at all.

France since the revolution had been riven by materialists on one side, who hated the Church and scoffed at the piety of ordinary people, and faithful Christians on the other. So the Lord raised up the small against the great. Think of the poor parish priest Saint John Vianney, patron saint of students who have trouble with their exams. Think of Bernadette.

And think of the thousands and millions of people who came to Lourdes. Think of the spiritual miracle of conversion of heart. Which is more difficult, to heal a clotted artery, or to soften a lifelong hardening of the heart in sin? Even in the earliest days, sinners came to Lourdes to sneer, and left in tears of joyful repentance.

The fact is, we all need the water from Lourdes. It isn't like the Ganges, one of the most polluted rivers in the world, but which harbors a germ that eats the germs on your flesh. Lourdes water has no such germs. Or it does have germs: the germinal seeds of faith, hope, and charity. Lourdes is available to us at all times. Christ the Healer is ready with the living water. We have only to submit, and to ask—and not heed what the scoffers will say. Some of them too will one day come down to the everlasting spring.

Teacher to the Nation

The scene is the Basilica of Saint Mark, in Milan, in 1874. The church is thronged, as it had been at the beloved man's funeral one year ago. Now the man's friend, his hair quite gray, stands on a dais before a vast orchestra and choir, and in quick and tremulous gestures he raises his arms and brings them down, rising and falling again and again, as the words thunder as if from heaven:

Dies irae, dies illa,
Solvet saeclum in favilla,
Teste David cum Sybilla!

The music rains down like that final fire that will dissolve the world. Yet the man is not angry. The choristers do not sing with fear. For one passionate half-hour they perform that sequence from the Mass for the Dead. It is only one part of the performance. There are the *Kyrie* and the *Sanctus* and the other prayers; the *Agnus Dei*, with a duet of sopranos soaring heavenward in appeal: *Agnus Dei, qui tollis peccata mundi, dona eis requiem.*

The conductor is also the composer, Giuseppe Verdi, the greatest genius of opera the world has known. Verdi had been raised Catholic and was an Italian patriot. So was the man who lay in his coffin in San Marco, in honor of whom Verdi composed his stupendous work of sacred opera. His name was Alessandro Manzoni, the greatest Italian writer of the 19th century, a loyal son of the Church, and to this day a beloved teacher to the nation.

What is enlightenment?

It would not have been so, if mere human beings had had their way. As I write, I'm looking at a painting of the young Alessandro. He is tall, with a long face, a shock of black hair, and pensive, intelligent eyes. In the wrong place, at the wrong time, he could have done great harm to himself, to others, and to the Church.

And he was indeed in the wrong place, at the wrong time. When he was a youth, he joined his divorced mother in Paris, in the fashionable salons, where men divided their days between indulging their intellects in falsehood, called reason, and their bodies in debauchery, called liberty. *Tear down the unspeakable thing!* Voltaire had cried, meaning the Church, and Alessandro agreed. It was convenient to agree.

But God had other plans for him. He married a pious Protestant girl, and in 1810, at the age of twenty-five, Alessandro Manzoni was present at her reception into the Catholic Church. From then till the day of his death, Manzoni dedicated himself, his intellect, and his art to Christ, the Church, his beloved Italy, and the poor.

For he hadn't forgotten everything from those salons. Pagans often speak more wisely than they know. The French had rebelled against the arbitrary abuse of power; and no one in Italy wrote with more fire against that than did Manzoni. French intellectuals had taken up the cause of the poor; and the hero and heroine of Manzoni's greatest work, *The Betrothed*, are but a poor young tailor, Renzo, and his promised spouse, Lucia. Manzoni was not a sentimentalist. He saw that reason brought light, but reason led to God, who *is* light. Enlightenment without God is red in tooth and claw: men will but more efficiently tear one another to ribbons. The Church led men to the true light.

Night, and a pistol

Another scene.

It is night, in a castle atop a mountain overlooking the town of Lecco. A man sits in his study. He is not young. His life is etched upon his face: a life of will, the exercise of power, an almost ascetic disdain for common pleasures, a keen intellect wasted. He is holding a girl in a room below. He has kidnapped her from a convent in Lecco, where she was hiding from a local nobleman, Don Rodrigo. She was promised in marriage to a peasant, a young tailor. Why has he done this? What is this Don Rodrigo to him?

The man's name arouses such fear that no one dares to breathe it. He is *L'Innominato:* "The

Unnamed." His own servants and henchmen tremble when he comes before them. And the girl... if only she had tried the ways of women! A leer, a pout, something to scorn, something impure; but she knelt before him, and she promised to pray for him.

"You have had a mother, my lord!" she cried. "Think of my mother. What have I done to you, my lord? Why will you not let me go home to my mother?" Her innocence disarmed him. Her innocence did more than that.

He takes a pistol out of its case and lays it before him on the desk. It is loaded. He cocks it, uncocks it, and cocks it again. A wasted life, a life of wickedness, and from that wickedness no joy, but only darkness visible. And if he dies, no one will pity him.

So it goes through the night, when in the early dawn he hears sounds from far below. Bells? The neighing of horses? The chatter of happy people? What is that life from which he has shut himself out?

The Unnamed descends.

Reader, do you want to know what happens? Do you want to be there when this lifelong criminal, this terrible man feared by everyone and weighted down by sin upon sin, descends the mountain? Why are the bells ringing? Who has come to town? You must read *The Betrothed.*

Hanging in the balance

Another scene. The plague has struck Lombardy—plague after famine. The saintly Cardinal of Milan, Federico Borromeo, has emptied his coffers for the relief of the poor. He has also built an asylum for the sufferers—a *lazaretto.* There, priests and nuns do all they can to feed the sick, to tend to them, to give them consolation, to protect their children, and to bury the dead. One hundred of the cardinal's priests will die in the effort.

One of those, Fra Cristoforo, is standing by the bed of a dying man. It is, or was, an aristocrat, Don Rodrigo by name. The man is raving in a fever. He cannot understand what is said to him. He appears to be dying in his wickedness.

Also standing there is a young tailor, Renzo. The dying man is his worst enemy. He had stolen his bride-to-be, and now she is dying somewhere in this vast field of sickness, or is already dead.

He had sworn vengeance. "If I don't find her," he had cried, "I'll sure find someone else! In Milan, or in his filthy palace, or in the devil's own house, I'll find that swine who separated us! My Lucia, twenty months it's been, she'd have been mine, and if we had to die, at least we'd die together. But if he's still alive and I find him"—but the priest had cut him short.

Not with easy words. Death and judgment everywhere, and hell gaping wide! "Wretched sinner!" cried the priest, "look and see who chastises man, who judges and is not judged! Who plies the lash and who pardons! But you, worm of the earth, you want to deal out justice. You know what justice is, you!" And with such words, not balm but a purifying fire, he scored the soul of the boy, stripped away its selfishness, and left it bare to the dreadful medicine of God.

So they stand, the boy and the priest; the one a young survivor, the other about to die of the illness himself. And there in bed lies the evil man, the source of so much misery.

"For four days he has been as you see. No sign of consciousness," says the priest. "Maybe the Lord is ready to grant him an hour of reconciliation, but he wants you to pray for him; maybe he wants you and that innocent girl to pray; maybe he reserves his grace for your prayer alone, the prayer of a heart in pain, but resigned to the pain. Maybe the salvation of this man—and your own—depends upon you, hangs upon one impulse of pardon, of compassion—of love!"

What happens then? You must read *The Betrothed.*

Where is his like?

When Alessandro Manzoni died at the age of eighty-eight, all of Italy mourned. If you go to Lecco you can see in the Piazza Manzoni a monumental sculpture of the author, an old man seated with a book, his head slightly tilted, as in kindly thought about the grandeur and the folly of man, and the love of God that overcomes all wickedness. Or you may go to Milan, to the Cimitero Monumentale, where he is entombed. Or you may ask schoolchildren about Renzo and Lucia, and they will be happy to tell you things; because in Italy, *The Betrothed* is not just studied. It is beloved.

No one now where English is spoken stands as Manzoni did for the Italians. But he would never want us to end with praise of himself. The true and only man, as Manzoni knew, was Christ. So I will end with a verse from Manzoni's hymn in honor of the Resurrection:

He is risen: his sacred head
Rests upon the cloth no more;
He is risen: to one side
Of the lonely sepulcher
Lies the shroud he tossed away:
Like a strong man flushed with wine
Wakes the Lord upon this day.

Sign of Beauty, Sign of Glory

Well was it called the Place of the Skull. Gray-white limestone, rugged and creased, barren of life, you would suppose; but for the stunted pines at the base, the wild grasses with no name, a deep blue iris here and there poking out bravely from the vertical face, and the coo of doves nesting in the clefts of the rock.

An old woman hobbled up the stony way to the bald top of the hill, leaning upon a stick. She was dressed in grave simplicity, but the cortege of soldiers gave witness that she was a lady of importance. "Augusta," said an old man, darting a glance from side to side, expecting to catch sight of someone in the shadows, "this is the place."

"You are not lying to us?"

"I am in fear of my life, Augusta."

"You will not betray the Lord, Judas?"

"*Domina*, I did not name myself. This is the place."

The old woman looked about. Nearby stood a temple that Hadrian, emperor of Rome two hundred years past, had built, as if in scorn of the love that here was made manifest, here and nowhere else. It was a temple to the goddess of love, Aphrodite.

"Our people have known of the place and kept it secret," said Judas. "It is here, buried under earth and stones."

"We shall see," said the old woman, and she raised her cane toward the soldiers. They were carrying picks and shovels. "Dig here," she said.

Nothing but skulls

The old woman had seen much in her time. She was but a girl, helping her father work the busy inn he kept in the old city by the gulf; shipmen and camel drovers, day after day, barbarians to the north, pagans all round, and Christians, those strange people, trying to honor their Lord in peace, yet willing to die for him when the persecutions came.

One day he showed up, Constantius the military commander, nicknamed the Paleface, the man she honored and loved. Husband and wife then went west, to live not in palaces but in camps along the Danube and the cold Rhine, keeping the Germans on the far side. She had seen many a man die on a cross. She bore an only son to him, named Little Constantius, that is, Constantinus.

So long ago it was. Constantius was true and not true to his name. He was constant in his love for the empire, constant in courage, constant in just administration of the laws. He was fair to Christians when such fairness was frowned upon. And he was constant in ambition, so when the chance came for him to be named praetorian prefect of the West, he took it, and abandoned his wife, marrying the daughter of the co-emperor Maxentius.

Constantius became emperor himself, but he would not wear that title long, dying in York after victories against the men with the painted bellies—the Picts. His wife herself had lived for a long time in that faraway island, Britain, in the company of her son. He too was a fighter, and an ambitious man.

Oh, the emperors, they come and go, she thought. She had seen enough of them for one lifetime. Hadrian too, he came and went.

"Nothing but rubble so far, *Domina*," said the centurion. "Rubble and skulls."

"Let the skulls be. We are searching for life, not death. Keep digging."

So they did.

In this sign you shall conquer

Who rules the world?

She saw in her mind's eye the great Diocletian, whom she had known. In his late years, people said that you had to lie on your face when you approached him, calling him "*Dominus et Deus,*" as if he were some god out of the god-besotted east.

She smiled and shook her head. The man himself did not believe a bit of it. All stage, all show. He enjoyed governing, which he was remarkably good at, and gardening also. In his old age he gave up the former so he could better enjoy the latter. Before that, his underling had persuaded him to persecute the Christians, which he did, as he did all things, with real efficiency.

"Artichokes would have been better," she said to herself.

"*Domina*?"

"Ah, centurion, I was thinking about an emperor. Anything yet?"

"Rubble is all."

"Almost all," she said.

Rubble was what they left of the church in her father's city. By then she was in Britain with Constantinus. She was making her deliberate way toward Christ. She had seen too much of the world to be hasty. A Greek philosopher could oil the world with his words; and oil meant money and power. The dark priests of Britain terrified the people; and terror meant money and power. Augustus and Rome were god and goddess, and they were nothing without money and power. Christ was not only different. He was that whole world turned upside down.

"Mother," said Constantinus one day, "I have had a dream."

They were outside of Rome, and her son was fighting for control over the west. Mother and son had been nudging one another along the Christian way. He told her the dream. It was of a shining cross in the heavens, with the words *en Toutoi Nika*: In this, be victorious.

"It is a sign of shame," he said. "A scandal to the Jews, and folly to the Greeks," said she.

"Death and defeat," he said.

"Life and victory."

"What does it mean?" he said.

"It means that the world is not ruled as men have thought."

"I shall have my men bear this sign upon our banners."

The dream indeed came true. And she, Helena, the humble daughter of an innkeeper, became Augusta, the most powerful woman in the world.

"*Lignum, lignum!*" cried the soldiers. "The wood of life," said she.

How can we tell?

Helena could have spent her later years as Diocletian did, gardening, and enjoying the wealth of an empress. Or that was what she did, in fact. She enjoyed that wealth by giving it away, endowing and planting churches wherever she went, in Rome and Trier and now in Palestine.

She took a gold coin from a fold of her garment. She looked at it with an old woman's ironic eye. "I haven't looked like that in many years," she thought, seeing her stamped bust upon it, with full cheeks and braided hair and a coronet. "Augusta," it read, while on the reverse stood an allegory of Security, holding an olive branch. No security but in Christ, she thought.

"Augusta," said the centurion, as if short of breath. "We have found three of them. Three posts and three beams."

The old woman hobbled to the edge of the cavity, fell to her knees, and peered down. Five or six sweating men, stripped to the waist, looked up to her, holding their picks upright and backing away, in dread, from the planks. For a few moments no one said a word. A dove cooed from the rocks above.

"How can we tell?"

Helena turned about. "Judas!" she cried.

The old Jewish man stood near.

"Do you know which one it is?"

"No, Augusta. But," he said, with all the courage he could muster, "I know a woman who is dying of typhus. Perhaps," he said, but the empress interrupted him. "Bring her here!"

That was how they knew they had found the true cross of Christ, when the dying woman was cured. This Judas did not go and hang himself from a tree. He did not ask for thirty pieces of silver for his services. He was baptized, and took the name Kyriakos (Latin *Cyriacus*), meaning "Belonging to the Lord."

Helena built a chapel nearby, and several other great churches in the Holy Land. For many years, the bulk of the cross stood there. But as soon as it was found, relics were sent round the Christian world for veneration. Scoffers say that if all the relics of the cross were gathered up, it would be as big as a battleship. That is complete nonsense. One scholar has estimated that the bulk of all the relics would amount to about one-fortieth of a cross of pine wood weighing a hundred and fifty pounds. Think how light a splinter is, and how a thousand of those put together would still be as light as a few feathers.

The world turned upside down

In 313, Constantine gave legal recognition to the Christian faith, and in 380 Theodosius made it the official religion of the empire. "My Kingdom is not of this world," said Jesus, but did that mean that man's pursuit of the common good in this life was to have nothing to do with his pursuit of the ultimate good, the vision of God in the communion of saints? After the son of Saint Helena, Christian missionaries could freely go to the ends of the earth, as Jesus had commanded, baptizing all nations in the name of the Father, and of the Son, and of the Holy Spirit.

Then it was that Europe as we know it was born. And slowly, slowly, into dull and muddle-headed man, came the idea that power was manifest in meekness, strength in love, and life in the Death and Resurrection of Jesus.

Be Not Afraid

"I won't, I won't!" cried the woman, writhing in the agony of nightmare. Her husband shook her gently.

"Wanda," he said, as she opened her eyes and began to recognize where she was. It was her home. There stood a crucifix upon the wall. Her rosary was on her nightstand.

"Oh, Andrzej!" she said, weeping. "The dreams—will I ever be free of them?"

"In God's good time," he said. He didn't want to suggest more. He was a philosopher, and she was the psychiatrist.

"I shall write them down," she said.

But no dream could be as terrible as the reality had been. She and her friend, a girl named Krysia, had drawn together in a friendship of suffering and faith. They had promised each other not to become like brute beasts, just because they were starving. They didn't blame the other girls and women. All our own virtues are God's gifts to us.

The place was Ravensbrück, a concentration camp. Wanda had been arrested for passing messages to the Polish resistance against the Nazis. What the guards did to women there in return for an extra scrap of fat or brown bread, we needn't guess. Wanda and Krysia kept themselves from it. But the godless intellectuals were worse than the guards, and from them they had no recourse.

"Be still," the doctor growled, "or it will only hurt worse." The long needle pierced her flesh and muscle and penetrated the bone. Slowly, with detached and clinical precision, he injected bacteria into Wanda's marrow. And on he went to the next human experiment. The Nazis were scientists, after all. They wanted to see what would happen to the bacteria under certain conditions.

They caused open wounds and then injected them with pus, causing the women agonies of fever and pain, often ending in a horrible death. Wanda too had died after four years at Ravensbrück. Or so the woman doctor thought when she looked at her motionless body. "Number 7709," she said. "Throw her on the pile."

That was where she lay, in a heap of corpses, when Krysia saw her fingers twitch. That saved her life. It was 1945, and she was twenty-four years old.

The good bishop

Wanda Półtawska vowed to God that if she survived, she would become a doctor, a healer. She earned her doctorate in psychiatry, and ministered especially to survivors of the camps, and to children who had been abused. At this time she and her husband became close friends with a young bishop in Kraków, named Karol Wojtyła.

Imagine in your mind's eye the athletic bishop, surrounded by young people, both men and women, on one of his outings into the country, hiking, skiing, and rowing. He urges them to embark upon the true adventure of love, and for most of them that will be made manifest in marriage. The Półtawskas are there too. Their conversations help him to sharpen his views on what he will later call *the theology of the body.*

For the body, male and female, has meaning. It is not inert stuff to be experimented upon, even when you yourself are the experimenter. If you violate that meaning, you violate yourself. It would be like amputating a healthy limb—or like injecting disease into healthy tissue. Dr. Półtawska had learned by experience what man can sink to when he loses the sense that his body is meant for holiness. Man—woman—is no mere thing for man's use. Young people can be called to heroism and holiness, or else they will sink to hedonism. There is no real third choice.

When Pope Paul VI issued the encyclical *Humanae vitae* (1968), affirming what the Church had taught for two thousand years, the thought of Bishop Wojtyła was there, and also the thought of the woman who had seen where a fundamental materialism must lead. When all the world had given way, one institution, the Church, stood against the flood.

The Italian priest and the French doctor

But Doctor Półtawska would not have survived to advise the bishop were it not for a remarkable priest in the hills of southern Italy.

It is 1962. He has been handed a message: "Venerable Father," it begins, and begs him to pray for a mother of four girls, a survivor of the camps, now stricken with cancer and in danger of her life, "that God may extend his mercy to this woman and her family in the presence of the Most Blessed Virgin." It is signed, "Most obligated in Christ, Karol Wojtyła."

"To such a request one must not say no," said Padre Pio.

When the surgeons went to remove the cancer in her throat, it was gone, simply gone. It had been devoured by grace. Dr. Półtawska went to San Giovanni Rotondo to find out for herself what had happened. She had never met Padre Pio before. When she arrived he was in the chapel saying Mass. She entered, and he paused, looking upon her as if to say, "It was for you I prayed."

This was one of the miracles that led to Padre Pio's canonization.

Dr. Półtawska knew from the camps that a human life cannot be placed in the balance with any other good upon earth. Doctors therefore must be in the business of life, not death. We must choose.

We cannot avoid the choice. After the war, she wrote, "a group of doctors [were] condemned to death for crimes against humanity, because of euthanasia and experimentation on humans. Another group of doctors created a hospital within the Warsaw Ghetto and when the Ghetto was closed all the patients died of starvation. The doctors remained with their patients and died with them. The two groups of doctors had been colleagues before the war."

She delivered those words in 2004, at the ten-year anniversary for the Association of Friends of Professor Jérôme Lejeune, the doctor who had discovered the chromosome that causes Down Syndrome, and who had fought manfully for those children and their right to live. Dr. Półtawska, Dr. Lejeune, and the bishop, now Pope John Paul II, formed a powerful troika for life. She recalled going to Lejeune's workshop in France, and finding there the humblest things, "broken bits and pieces for mending dolls, and watering cans, and an old iron. For him," she said, "everything, no matter how useless, was an object of beauty." How much more than dolls, then, are human lives!

In the midst of life

It is May 13, 1981. Pope John Paul has just announced the founding of the Pontifical Institute for Studies on Marriage and Family, with Dr. Lejeune as its president, and Dr. Półtawska on the governing board. He has lunch with Lejeune and his wife, who return to Paris that day. A few hours later, a Turkish gunman, put up to it by the Soviets, shoots and nearly kills the pope. That same night, Jérôme Lejeune lies ill in a hospital in Paris.

The pope, entrusting himself to Our Lady of Fatima, survives, and lives to see the end of the Soviets and their Polish puppets. Man's history lies not in some impersonal historical force, but in the providence of God. Someone should have told the Soviets that. Dr. Lejeune survives. The Institute continues.

So does the Pontifical Academy for Life, also dear to the pope's heart. It was founded in 1994, on February 11, the feast of Our Lady of Lourdes. John Paul had intended that Jérôme Lejeune be its president too, but on April 3, Dr. Lejeune passed away suddenly. Wanda Półtawska was having breakfast with the pope when the news was brought to him.

Sometimes it seems as if the history of the Church is a series of hair's-breadth escapes, of a man clinging by a branch to the side of a cliff, or grabbing hold of a spar as the ship he had been on goes down to the bottom of the sea. Life in Christ may be filled with joy or suffering or both, but one thing it never is, and that is dull. Nor are the persons in the Church's drama: the diminutive woman doctor who healed the nightmares of others; the cheerful Frenchman and his care for the least among us; the Polish patriot who became pope and braved a secular world to his right and his left; a quiet monk in the crossroads to nowhere.

Death is all around us, but we are in the midst of life.

One more thing about Dr. Półtawska. She is still with us on earth, as I write these words. I can't go on social media to find Thomas Aquinas or even Jérôme Lejeune, but I have found Wanda Półtawska. Her face is that of an old Polish grandma, her eyes crinkled with many years of kindliness. I see a monstrance with the Blessed Sacrament. She writes, in Polish, about how good it is to go every day to be in the presence of the Lord God in the tabernacle, and to talk to him. He answers, she says, not with a shout, but in silence.

Jewels for the Lord

A man lies back against a wooden cradle, high in the apse of the ancient church of Saint Clement in Rome. Before him stands the scooped-out round of a half-dome. Most of it is bare plaster. It's marked in rough strokes of black paint, a welter of shapes, hard to identify, except for the cross in the center, which is beginning to take form and color by his sure hand and keen eye.

"Master," says a boy, sitting upon the scaffolding, "why is heaven made of gold, when the sky is blue?"

The master takes from him a small gold tile, less than an inch square. He smiles a little but does not take his eye from the cross.

"Not this one," he says. "A little brighter, more yellow and less red." The boy scans a floor of tiles spread out before him, one by one, according to color and brilliance—gold and red, rich green and blue, pale pink and white. They are marble, jasper, garnet, lapis, onyx, and glass, and some of the tiles are overlaid with gold leaf beaten as thin as air. He picks out one that seems to shine with its own light.

"Excellent," says the master, fixing it in the plaster, right up against the dark wood of the cross.

"In a hundred years, son, what will happen to the gold?"

"Nothing," says the boy. "Gold doesn't rust."

"In a thousand years?"

"Nothing."

"That's why we use gold for heaven. It's filled with light, and it will never pass away."

The boy falls silent. Patience is all. His master is kind, and won't forget to teach him the art. His own fingers will soon be pressing gold tiles into the skies that show forth the cross, while the master works the subtle colors for Jesus and Mary and John. And the master will let him work on one of the smaller figures, a branch, a leaf, perhaps one of the birds—a peacock, maybe!

Living stones

Christians didn't invent mosaics. You can find them wherever you find colored stones. If you go to Pompeii, you can see somebody's mosaic for the pavement of his house. It's of a snarling black brute, and it reads *CAVE CANEM*—Beware of the Dog. Go to an old Roman bath, and you'll see pavements with dolphins, friendly to man, and fish, and sea-gods and goddesses.

But the Church raised the mosaic to a height never attained before or since. I'm not talking about technical skill. The *matter* of the art raised up the *material* to the divine. We ourselves, says Saint Peter, are like living stones raised up to be a spiritual house. That's not by our effort, but by the work of Christ.

He is the stone which the builders rejected that has become the cornerstone. Can stones come to life?

Look at the great apse at Saint Clement. Nothing in art can compare to it. Your first impression is of a whole world of gold and green: everything ablaze with life. I can't describe it all; it would be like making a catalogue of the universe. A little will have to do.

Jesus is in the center, upon the cross, which is now the Tree of Life. Twelve doves, the Apostles, move along the beams. Mary and John stand below, one on each side. But the cross has taken root! Its base has blossomed into an acanthus bush, symbol of immortality. You can see the acanthus on the capital of any Corinthian column. Here the scheme of glory is reversed: the cross is the column, its base is the acanthus, and it brings life back to a world given over to sin and death.

And what happens to the bush? It bursts forth into glory, and is not consumed or even contained. "I am the vine, you are the branches," said Jesus, and sure enough the branches of the tree of life cover the dome with their lush and complicated triple curls. They bear fruit, too: the fruit of holiness, of saints, of the New Jerusalem.

Are we there too, ordinary people? Yes, we are. Here are a couple of men with sheep and goats. Here's a peasant woman feeding her chicks, with a delightfully gaudy rooster looking on. Peacocks, lilies, roses, baskets of fruit, even a naked cherub riding a happy dolphin.

Living water

Most of the time you'll see the blood of Christ flowing down the cross to bring life to the earth beneath, with a skull at the base, for Golgotha, but also for death: it is Adam's skull, man's skull.

"Can these bones live?" said God to the prophet Ezekiel in the valley of the dry bones. Yes, they can, in Christ. So the artist at Saint Clement shows a flood of water gushing forth from the base of the cross: the four rivers of paradise. The second Adam has flung open the gates of a new Eden.

"I will give you living water," said Jesus to the woman at the well. Living water is not stagnant but rushing; not brackish but fresh. It is new water—ever new. Who longs for such water? We all do. So the artist has portrayed deer drinking from the water, careless of the tail of the dead serpent nearby. "As the deer longs for flowing streams," says the psalmist, "so longs my soul for you, O God."

Blue becomes the dominant color there, a rich blue and white. That is not only for the water we need for our lives here and now. The artist is always thinking of eternity. He is thinking of the vision of Saint John, and the river of the water of life, that flows from the side of the throne of God and the

Lamb, with the tree of life on either side. We are made to thirst for that water.

We thirst for the sight of God, the living God. Only such a thirst can raise the mind and heart of man beyond himself. And only a vision of the whole of life, from its beginning when God commanded the light into being to its end and beyond, in the new heaven and new earth, can have animated all those artists whose names we do not know to fashion works that otherwise man can never accomplish, because he never conceives them in the first place.

"Another gold, my boy," says the master.

Never like this

"Master," says the boy, knitting his brows, "what do the words mean?" He can serve at the altar, so he knows some Latin, but he isn't sure of these. It's a big inscription, running along the base of the dome.

"Ah, the bishop himself composed those."

"Composed?"

"Verses, my boy. Poetry. I'm not very good at it, but let me give it a try." He reads it out, keeping the syllables distinct and putting the accents where they belong:

EC-cle-si-AM CHRIS-TI VI-TI si-mi-LA-bi-mus
IS-TI:
DE LIG-NO CRU-CIS, Ja-co-BI DENS, IG-na-ti-I-QUE
IN-SUP-RA SCRIP-TI re-qui-ES-CANT COR-po-re
CHRIS-TI,

QUAM LEX A-REN-TEM, SED CRUX fa-cit ES-se vi-REN-TEM.

The boy's eyes grow wide. He guesses a little, but the rest is a mystery. "It means this," says the Master. "We have likened the Church of Christ to this vine, which the Law made withered and dry, but the cross has caused to be green with life again. That's the first and last lines. The ones in the middle say that we've placed some wood of the cross under the body of Christ here, along with a tooth from Saint James and Saint Ignatius."

"Teeth!"

"Sure, right underneath these tiles, here and here."

"Like hidden treasure," says the boy. "But what kind of poetry is that?" he says, trying to count the syllables.

"Very old, very old. I can't tell how old. Pagans made it."

"They didn't believe in Jesus."

"No, they didn't."

"But we use their poetry."

"We use their roads, don't we? And they did this too," says the master, motioning toward the tiles.

The boy surveys the colors again. Light from the window strikes them and makes them glimmer as if alive.

"But not like this," says the boy.

"Never like this."

Light everlasting

If you look at the top of the dome at Saint Clement, you will see Christ the Ruler of the world, with symbols of the evangelists to his left and right. His hand is raised in blessing, with two fingers extended, for he is true Man and true God, both. Below him is a medallion bearing the Chi-Rho symbol for his name, and the Alpha and the Omega, for he is the one who is and who was and who is to come, the first and the last, the Almighty.

You can find mosaics all over the Christian world, from the Caucasus mountains in the east to Portugal in the west, and then on to the new world. They express, better than any other form of art, both the solid weightiness of the faith and its light-bearing power. It is as if light itself had heft: blocks of light, pillars of light, arches and domes of light.

If you say, "We can still have mosaics without the Church," you'd be right, but what would be the point of it? We have gold still, but without the Church, without faith in Christ, to what would we apply that gold?

Let us then strive to see as that master of Saint Clement did, long ago. For he saw not by his own light, but by Christ, the light of the world.

King of the Northmen

"What is your name, young man?" said the archbishop.

"Sir, I am Olaf, son of Harald," said the boy. "Harald the king." "Olaf the son of Trygve was a great friend of the Christian faith. Will you be like the man whose name you bear?"

"I wish to learn," said the boy.

"Do you see this heap of burnt beams and stone?" They were walking near a church, newly built, but ruins lay nearby. "It once was a great cathedral. Our people destroyed it."

"I don't understand," said the boy. "Why would they destroy their own church?"

"I mean *our people*," said Robert, Archbishop of Rouen. "Men of the north. Have you been on many raids, Olaf Haraldsson?"

The boy furrowed his brow. "Of course," he cried. "I love to fight!" "Do you wish to put on the full armor of God?" The archbishop stopped and gestured toward the great port city. "What kind of life is it, your raiding, your putting seacoast towns to the torch, when you go back to Norway and spend your time with goats and pigs and endless feuds with other raiders and sons of raiders? What is it for?"

"I don't know," said the boy.

"Look at me," said Robert. "We Normans are of your blood. It is time you joined us in the Christian faith, the true faith. It is time for more than raids and feuds. You are the son of a king. What is it to be a king?"

Olaf would try to solve that riddle for the rest of his life. But in 1010, at the age of fifteen, he was baptized in Normandy. So began his remarkable career of fighting for a unified and free nation, Norway, and for the faith he accepted in Rouen.

Sorting out the nations

"Sire," said the young man, "I can take down those armies, if you wish."

The English king shook his head. His name was Ethelred, and he would be called "the Unready," not because he wasn't prepared, but because he was sometimes given bad advice. So he hesitated.

"Young man, the Danes hold the bridge. You can't get near them. They drop great stones from that height. They have crushed several of our ships. We must storm them from the land." A disastrous proposition, but Ethelred could think of nothing else. That, or surrender.

The River Thames flowed on in its power past the city of London.

"Let the responsibility be mine, and the loss be ours," said the lad, turning to his fair-haired countrymen. He bore a grudge against the Danes for having murdered his father. He craved action, too, and had been on many a Viking raid along the coasts of the North Sea and the Baltic Sea.

"Go then, and God be with you."

"Which god?" asked the lad. The men he fought beside did not all agree. Ethelred shook his head. "There is only one."

"I know it," said the boy. So the lad Olaf instructed his fellows from Norway what to do. They would not hurl spears or shoot arrows at the Danes. That would be suicide. Instead they rowed in their several ships up toward the bridge. Each ship was covered by a "roof" of planks bound up with hazel branches and supported by pillars underneath, so that the boulders would rebound from them without harm.

When they were under the bridge, Olaf had them loop iron cables around each of the great piers.

That done, he cried, "Row, my men! Row!" And the river's current and the men's strong arms wrenched the piles from their beds, and what with all the soldiers and their boulders atop, the bridge gave way—London Bridge, falling down, as it is remembered in the nursery rhyme. The Danes drowned in the Thames or fled, and the English rebels gave way and acknowledged Ethelred as their king. So continued the historical movement that would leave Danes in charge in Denmark, and the Normans and English in charge of England.

One of the Norse poets sang out, "Odin makes our Olaf win!" But Olaf did not believe in Odin.

The lawgiver

"It was the king's custom," says the author of the saga of Olaf, "to rise betimes in the morning, put on his clothes, wash his hands, and then go to the church and hear the matins and morning Mass. Thereafter he went to the Thing-meeting, to bring people to agreement with each other, or to talk of one or the other matter that appeared to him necessary." The *Thing* was what the people of the north called assemblies for the common good, the redress of grievances, and the settling of disputes. Olaf, crowned king in 1015 at the age of twenty, sought out all the "things" up and down the coast of Norway, to bring together the petty princes and landholders, and to see that one law would prevail in a united nation. Says another poet:

The king, who at the helm guides
His warlike ship through clashing tides,
Now gives one law for all the land—
A heavenly law, which long will stand.

It was light, breaking into darkness. Let's not be too romantic about the Viking culture. The great novelist of Norway, Sigrid Undset, tells what might happen during a time of plague, when some of the Norse in desperation slid back into their pagan practices: the ritual sacrifice of a small boy, to placate the dark gods beneath the earth. The Vikings were skilled sailors, brave and ferocious in battle, more admirable in defeat than in victory, for they believed that a man should rather die on the field after his chief had fallen than flee and save his life. They had much going for them, but they did not have the truth.

And we must not confine these Northmen to Scandinavia. They swarmed over all the seas, raiding ports from Sicily to Russia to Ireland and Iceland. They traveled overland and sailed down the great Russian rivers to Constantinople. Waves of German pagans and heretics had once toppled Roman rule in the west, to usher in several centuries of cultural decline. This last wave of German pagans acted as a brake against a Europe ready to burst out into one of the greatest cultural flowerings in the history of the world. The last pier of the old bridge would fall and a new bridge would be built up in its place: the Vikings would accept the Christian faith. King Olaf was a central figure at the change.

Let one story suffice as an example. The farther north you went in Norway and the farther up the mountains, the more likely were the people to cling to their old gods. So Olaf went with his bishop to a place called Gudbrandsdal, governed by a man named Gudbrand, who had many warriors loyal to him. In a skirmish along the way, Olaf captured Gudbrand's son, but spared him and sent him home to his father, telling him that he would be coming soon to bring the law and the true faith. Gudbrand scoffed, but that night he dreamed of a man surrounded with light, who warned him that if he rose against King Olaf, he would get no glory of it, and his flesh would be meat for the ravens.

When Olaf arrived at Gudbrandsdal, the people looked askance. They were set in their ways. Said Gudbrand to Olaf, "We don't know anything about this God of yours whom we cannot see. But we can see our god, and you will see him too, mighty and terrible. But if your God is so great, let him make it a cloudy day tomorrow, without rain, so that we may meet again."

Olaf kept watch all night in prayer. The next day the weather was cloudy, without rain. Then one of Gudbrand's men challenged Olaf to ask God to make it clear and sunny the next day, so that they might fight, or be converted. Again Olaf kept watch and prayed.

The next day the people brought out their god, the hammer-throwing Thor, a huge hollow statue inlaid with silver and gold. "Where is *your* God, Olaf?" they taunted.

Olaf turned toward Kolbein, one of his men, armed with a big war-club. "When they look away from their idol, strike," he said. Then Olaf said to the people, "Your god is blind and deaf, and cannot even move unless somebody carries him. But our God is advancing in great light. Do you not see him?" He motioned toward the rising sun. The people turned to the east.

Then Kolbein struck. The idol was shattered, and from its hollow innards came forth mice and snakes. Gudbrand's people fled in terror. But Gudbrand, he was a practical man. "This idol cannot help us," he said. "We will accept your God." So did the rest of the people of that valley. Olaf left them some teachers of the faith, and Gudbrand himself built their church.

Exile and death

Olaf's measures were often severe, and powerful rivals, joining with his perennial enemy Canute of Denmark, drove him into exile in Russia. Olaf returned, and was slain at the battle of Siklestad in 1031. He was only thirty-six years old.

In a relatively short time, though, he had accomplished much, and the Norse people revered him as a patriot and a Christian king. Soon pilgrims came to visit his tomb in Trondheim, where many miracles were attributed to his intercession. He was canonized in 1164.

Doves in the Clefts of the Rock

"Mother, I will not let you do this! You're still too young to throw your life away!"

"Celse-Benigne," said the widow, a woman of gentle countenance but firm in stature, "do you want to keep me from the call of the good God?"

The boy was dressed as befitted a courtier of the king of France. He was a favorite at court, as he was gallant and brave, and he never would leave a friend in the lurch. That meant that when he grew up he would be embroiled in many *affaires d'honneur*, or what we would call duels. He was generous, impetuous, all made of fire. His mother loved him to distraction.

"I've settled our worldly matters, Celse-Benigne. You haven't been spending too much, have you?"

"No," said the son. "But this is madness! I won't let you go!" And he threw himself to the floor, lying across the threshold of what would become the first House of the Visitation. He wept.

The widow was deeply moved. "I am still a mother, after all," she said. But she stepped across him and entered the house. It was in Annecy, twenty miles south of Geneva.

The vision of a saint

Jane Frances, Baroness de Chantal, had made a vow of chastity to God after her husband died in a shooting accident, leaving her with four young children. That was in 1601. She longed for a spiritual director, and God granted her a vision of the man with whom she was to work until his death. She recognized him in the flesh in 1604: Saint Francis de Sales.

Recall that the followers of John Calvin had won over Switzerland and much of France, and in the gray city of Geneva there sounded no longer the bells of joy. Calvin had been a lawyer, and his theology followed the severity of his mind. It was manly, in a grim way; and neither the Swiss nor the French Huguenots could be won over by riches, laxity, and outward shows of religion. Francis de Sales had been made Bishop of Geneva, with his seat in Annecy. When he was a student he had almost lost his faith in despair at the thought that God might have predestined him to hell. But God brought him through that trial the more determined to delve deeply into *mercy*, to win the Calvinists back to the fold.

He and Jane Frances became close friends and collaborators. Her idea was to establish an order inspired by Mary's going to assist her elderly cousin Elizabeth when she was with child. They would not only visit the sick. They would take the infirm and the elderly *into their ranks*. Other orders of nuns followed rules that many women would find too taxing, physically; and some women simply did not feel moved to accept the severities. It was Mother de Chantal's inspiration to find a place for these women, and Francis de Sales' inspiration to found the new order upon a mild rule, establishing them as contemplatives rather than active in the world. He called them his "doves," from whose dove-cot would come unceasing prayer for the Church.

When Mother de Chantal died in 1641, there were eighty-six of those homes for doves, spread throughout France.

Bringing the heart into discipline

If the Sisters of the Visitation did not have to pray the full Divine Office every day, and did not subject themselves to great periods of fasting, that did not mean there was no discipline. Both Jane Frances and Francis de Sales believed that if these sisters were less able to endure trials of the flesh, so much the more determinedly should they mortify the spirit.

In her letters we find her always recommending virtues that we often neglect. "May God give us genuine humility, sweetness, and submission," she writes to another superior, "for with these virtues there is truth, but without them usually deception."

To a mistress of novices she says that we do well not to dwell on our feelings. "What does it matter if you are dense or stolid or over-sensitive? Anyone can see that this is all self-love seeking its satisfaction. For the love of God let me hear no more of it: love your own insignificance and the most holy will of God which has allotted it to you." When we are humble we can more easily open ourselves up to the love of our neighbor. Jane Frances returns to that charity again and again, recalling how Francis de Sales won men to the truth as much by humility as by learning. "If our Sisters really love their holy Founder," she says, "they will prove it not only by the attention and pleasure with which they read his writings, for all the world delights in them, but also by faithfully carrying out his teachings. [They should practice above all] that incomparable love and sweetness towards their neighbor, that profound humility and lowliness of which he was so great a lover, and which put him at enmity with all ostentation."

But she was also a woman of passionate charity, and she never hesitated to express her admiration for the love she found in others. To an angelic girl of eighteen years, Sister Claire-Marie-Françoise de Cusance, now known as Saint Stanisław Kostka of the Visitation, who at the time of the letter was dying of the plague, Jane Frances writes: "My dearest daughter: Your letter fills me with tender compassion, but it also gives me very real comfort, seeing how joyfully God is enabling you to make your passage through this life to him. You will love and adore him in an eternity of glory, for this is the only good that is worth setting our hearts upon." And she begs her for the great kindness of speaking of her to God when she sees him.

It was surely no coincidence that another Sister of the Visitation, Saint Margaret Mary Alacoque, would bequeath to the Church her visions and her devotions to the Sacred Heart of Jesus.

Family of souls

Jane Frances was always solicitous for the spiritual well-being of her children in the flesh, and that included her favorite, the scapegrace Celse-Benigne. So she writes to the young baron, who must live in a world of temptation: "I beseech you, my own beloved son, since your condition obliges you to row on the tempestuous sea of this world, try never to swallow its waters, but drink rather of those of divine grace, turning in all your needs with a loving, filial trust to that source of mercy." One year later the Baron died the death of a patriot and a Christian. On the morning of battle against the English in the Thirty Years' War, Celse-Benigne prepared his soul by confession and the Sacrament. He led a troop of courtiers defending the fortress of Saint-Martin-de-Ré, on the west coast of France. This he did for six bitter hours, his body punched full of holes—twenty-six pike wounds. He "breathed his last," wrote a contemporary, "in sentiments of the most sincere piety."

It was no small skirmish. The English were trying to foment rebellion among the Protestant Huguenots in nearby La Rochelle against the royal government of France. Their failure led them to withdraw from the more general war, and that ensured that France would remain Catholic.

Meanwhile, after the death of Francis de Sales, Jane Frances found another guardian in his younger friend, Saint Vincent de Paul. From the Apostle of Gentleness she thus went to the Apostle of Charity, and so near to one another were the hearts of those two men that Jane Frances found no loss and no difference in spiritual direction. It was a remarkable conjunction of three most fervent and blessed souls. Here Jane Frances writes to Vincent, on the arrival at Annecy of five of his priests: "Praised be our divine Savior who for his great glory and the salvation of many souls has brought your dear children happily here.... We look upon them as our true brothers, with whom, in simple openheartedness and confidence, we are as one, and they too feel this.... Truly they speak as if they were daughters of the Visitation."

One of the last letters she wrote before her death in 1641 was to another holy woman, Sister

Louise-Angelique de la Fayette, at the Visitation convent in Paris. She was to become the spiritual advisor to Catholic royalty across Europe, from the hapless Charles II and James II of England to Louis XIII and Louis XIV of France. To her the saint writes that she must restrain her desire to be confirmed in her growth in perfection, but rather wait upon God, performing her duties even "without sensible feeling," so that she will find the peace that comes from submitting wholly to God's designs, instead of insisting upon her own inclinations.

That was typical of both her motherly good sense and her deep humility. May we learn from her, and come to raise spiritual families in turn, to our own joy and the great glory of God.

The Heavens Declare the Glory of God

"You're the prince of music," said one fellow to another, as they took their ease in their native German tongue. The chatter of the crowds below floated up to them in the night. The place was Bath, where people came to take the waters for their health, but mainly to enjoy the high life of the English spa. "They love you more than they have loved anyone since our brilliant countryman Handel." "That is kind of you, Wilhelm," said his friend, a man in his late middle age. "Handel shall be my master." He had heard the *Messiah* for the first time, in England.

His friend Wilhelm Herschel himself had been a composer of some fame, but he gave it over for study in another kind of order, another counterpoint. He turned some dials to work a telescope atop his house. It was forty feet long. He had built it himself.

"Look here, Joseph," he said, and the old man bent over to peer through the eyepiece. "What do you see?"

"I see a disk of light. A star?"

"A world like ours, beyond Saturn, revolving about the sun."

"*Gott im Himmel!* What is its name?"

"I call it *Georgium sidus*, after our glorious king." That was George III. "An English king with German blood."

"Precisely."

Let there be light

Joseph Haydn left England in 1795 and settled in Vienna, but he kept in mind that meeting with the astronomer. Three years later, he burst forth with his most famous oratorio, *The Creation*, a musical and theological meditation on the first chapter of Genesis. When I first heard Haydn's interpretation of the verse, "And God said, Let there be light, and there was—LIGHT!"—with its movement from a C minor adagio to a sudden, overwhelming C major chord on that word LIGHT, sung out by the whole choral ensemble—I shivered, and knew why Haydn's German audience erupted into applause when they heard it at its debut.

Haydn's life was not always exemplary. He married badly, and his wife took a lover. He followed her lead some years later. In those days, in the "enlightened" salons and palaces of Europe, you could do that and not be scorned, so long as you weren't scandalous about it. But he never gave up his Catholic faith, and later in life he was chaste. He prayed the rosary before he sat down to compose, and he signed his manuscripts by giving honor to

God. I've seen one of the signatures: *Laus Deo et B. V. Ma. et om. s.tis*: "Praise be to God, and to the Blessed Virgin Mary, and to all the saints."

In 1808, when he was weak with age, the Viennese gave a concert in his honor, featuring *The Creation*. The singers came to the word LIGHT, and the people applauded, but Haydn from his chair bowed and pointed above, to remind them that true light comes from God alone. The old man's head swam whenever he sat at the piano, but he was still filled with musical ideas, struggling to get free. "I'm nothing but a living clavier," he said, sadly. He was more, of course. He'd become the embodiment of all that was best and most honorable in high culture. A few days before his death, Napoleon and his armies were shelling Vienna, and when some of the shells exploded nearby, Haydn cried out from the window to the frightened people. He told them not to worry, because where Haydn was, no harm would come to them. But the terror shook his constitution. Still, Napoleon was no barbarian. After he took the city, one of his officers came to Haydn's house to sing for him—from *The Creation*.

Creation nearly stifled

People nicknamed him "Papa Haydn," though he and his wife were childless. Yet he should have been a father. There was always something mirthful about him: listen to his "Surprise" symphony and try not to laugh while the musicians are playing their beautiful jests! Haydn's childhood might have been very happy, had he had no talent. His father and mother, devout Catholics, noticed early on that Joseph was a brilliant little boy. Herr Haydn couldn't read music, but he did play Austrian folk songs on the fiddle and the harp, and one day he noticed Joseph sawing away with one wooden stick upon another, in perfect time. The boy's treble, too, was pure and beautiful and right on pitch. A kinsman who heard him singing took him to Vienna to study. Of him, Haydn later said, "He gave me more slaps than gingerbread." He was six years old, and he never lived with his parents again.

At eight, we find him in a Viennese school, Saint Stephen's. You may have heard of the Vienna Boys' Choir—it is the choir of that school. It had a high reputation in Haydn's time too, but the master, Karl Georg Reuter, was a severe man, whose sole interest in the boy was his voice. He gave him no lessons in composition. Food was sparing, and that may be why Joseph remained small of stature, and why his voice did not drop until he was eighteen. One day Joseph had stayed indoors while the other boys were outside having a lovely snowball fight. His mind was lost in music. Frau Reuter had been going to the door to give the knife-sharpener a pair of shears, when Joseph cried, "Something's burning in the kitchen!" It was the last meager portion of goulash in the house. The lady left the shears on the table, and Joseph picked them up idly, snipping with them to hear the ring and the rhythm of the steel. When the boys came back in, rosy with exercise and fun, Joseph sneaked up behind another boy and, snip! Off went the lad's pigtail. That occasioned a boy-wrestling match, when Reuter came in.

"You must be punished," he said, reaching for his cane.

"There's no need for that," said Joseph. "I'm leaving!"

"Not till you are caned first," said the master.

Joseph did leave, and were it not for his genius, his tremendous energy, and his ability to work hard and long hours—twelve to fourteen a day, when he was a boy, on his own—we would never have heard of him. He said, years later, that he *had* to be original to survive. He had no one to imitate. So he created.

It's remarkable to consider how close we often came to having not Haydn, but darkness.

Good friend and honest man

What did Haydn do for the symphony? He created it. Modern chamber music? The same. His fame went round the world. In 1815, people in Boston, most of whom had never seen him, in the days before recording, founded the Handel-Haydn Society, which exists to this day. It was impossible to think of culture without music—without musicians in every town and city who could make the compositions real. It might then go to your head, to be so famous, but that doesn't seem to have happened to Haydn. He acknowledged his debts to others—to Carl Philip Emmanuel Bach for one, the great son of a composer greater still. And he attracted others by his warmth and enthusiasm. Beethoven was one of his pupils, and Mozart, much his younger, was his close friend. He wrote to the elder Mozart, assuring him of his son's genius: "Before God and as an honest man I tell you that your son is the greatest composer known to me either in person or by name; he has taste, and, furthermore, the most profound knowledge of composition."

The plain-spoken Mozart esteemed Haydn just as highly. One evening Mozart was present while one of Haydn's works was being performed, and a man in the audience could do nothing but complain.

"I wouldn't have done that," said the man.

"Nor I," said Mozart. "That's because neither you nor I could have thought of something so perfectly fitting."

Mozart once dedicated six quartets to Haydn, calling them his "six sons," and begging Haydn to treat them kindly, as a father. Haydn did better than that. When Mozart died, Haydn worked hard to establish his friend's reputation in England, where he was still unappreciated. He was "much my superior," said Haydn, and he added that if the world really knew how great Mozart's genius was, the nations would fight one another to claim for their own so precious a jewel. Then he wrote to Mozart's widow and offered to train up their two small sons in music. He kept that promise.

The joy of faith

"Hin ist alle meine Kraft," wrote the elderly Haydn, setting the words to a simple air, *"alt und schwach bin ich"*—"Gone is all my strength; I am old and frail." But there was nothing morose about him, at heart. Asked about the liveliness of *The Creation,* Haydn said he could not think of God other than as a being of boundless might and goodness. Such goodness, he said, filled him with such joy, he "could have written even a *Miserere* in *tempo allegro.*"

"I defy any Christian," wrote a critic and a friend of Haydn, "who has heard on Easter day a *Gloria* of this composer, to leave the church without feeling his heart expand with sacred joy." Perhaps someday we too may have that experience!

Protector of the Indians

It is winter, 1517. A priest in the prime of life, tanned into a permanent brown by his years in the sun of the Caribbean, stands before the young king of his native Spain, Charles I, also the Holy Roman Emperor. Charles is intelligent, broad-minded, unsentimental, a devout Roman Catholic committed to the good of his subjects, whether Flemish, German, Austrian, Spanish, or the Indians of the New World.

"I can hardly believe that Spanish men would be capable of such wickedness, Father," says the king, blushing.

"Your majesty, I saw it with my own eyes."

"We are bringing them the true faith, which will set them free."

"We are making slaves of them to line our furs with gold."

"Our settlers say otherwise."

"They have reason to say so."

"And you, Father Bartolomé, do you have no reason to speak ill of our settlers? They say you hate them more than you love the Indians."

"I won't justify myself," says the priest. It is his turn to blush. "Let that be between me and God. What I say is true."

The young king considers. He is not cruel. "All right, Father. What do you propose?"

A true peace

So began the lifelong quest of Bartolomé de las Casas to bring Christ to the Indians, along with means of life to protect them from the less scrupulous Spanish settlers, and from the more warlike tribes of their own lands. We shouldn't forget why Cortez with his few hundred men could conquer the Aztec empire so quickly. The Aztecs were hated by the peoples they had thrust beneath them. Think of the daily stain and stench of human blood, when a prisoner of the Aztecs would have his still-beating heart knifed out of his chest in honor of the sun god.

Las Casas' attempts to build self-sustaining agricultural centers took various forms. At first, when he saw that the Indian men could not bear the hard physical labor that farming with iron tools required, he recommended importing slaves from Africa, as prisoners of a just war. But he would change his mind about that, once he saw how badly the blacks were treated in turn. Don't make light of it when a man's conscience is wrung. People change their minds, sure, when it profits them, when it earns them a seat at the best table, or when it hurts their enemies and costs them nothing. It is rare that a man of authority will change his mind to his own harm, opening himself to scorn, slander, enmity, and isolation.

Las Casas thought that Charles might send Spanish peasants to Venezuela, furnishing them with tools for farming. There they would work with the Indians and avert the excesses of the large *encomiendas*—the plantations. That project fell to ruin when natives from the interior descended upon the new villages, burned them to the ground, stole the goods, and killed the Europeans. Las Casas still concluded that the Spanish were to blame.

He had his greatest success with a mission in the heart of Guatemala, what had been called the Land of War. The governor had promised not to set up any *encomiendas* there, if Las Casas could bring the Indians to the faith. He and his fellow Dominicans taught the Indians by means of Indians, merchants who had been baptized and who dared to enter that wilderness, singing hymns in the native tongues. With Spaniards, Las Casas was ruthless, but with the Indians he was forbearing and patient. When two notable chiefs were baptized, more Dominicans followed in Las Casas' steps, and the Land of War became known as *Verapaz,* "True Peace." So it is known to this day.

Battle of the friars

Much of man's sorry history is the strife of bad men: Octavian and Antony, Alexander and Darius. But the strife of holy men?

Following in the wake of Cortez came Franciscan friars, led by Father Toribio de Benavente, called *Motolinía* or "Poor Man" by the natives who saw him for the first time, shoeless and in his brown cloak. "It is the first word I have learned in this language," said he, and to make sure he wouldn't forget it, he took it as his name. The Indians were astonished to see Cortez the conqueror, whom they saw as a god, kneeling before such a man. But they grew to love Motolinía profoundly. By his own testimony, he baptized four hundred thousand Indians. When he died, the Indians mobbed his bier to tear off bits of clothing as relics.

Motolinía was, like many holy men who live among the poor, patient with the rich. He was unwilling to destroy the estates they had built at great risk and expense, even if they had employed Indians as slaves. Las Casas was, like other holy men who live among the poor, impatient with the rich and eager to enforce severities to atone for their grievous sins, even at the cost of destruction. Motolinía would baptize all who desired it, even if they didn't understand more than the outlines of the faith. Las Casas would not baptize anyone unless he was sure that the conversion was of the intellect as well as of the will.

In 1555, the elderly son of Francis attacked the elderly son of Dominic, urging that his old enemy be confined to a monastery for the good of his soul.

It wasn't that the Franciscan was blind to Spanish sins, or to Indian sins, for that matter. Motolinía had numbered Spanish oppression as one of the ten plagues of the New World. But he and his fellows favored baptizing as many Indians as possible, particularly when they saw them dying of smallpox and other diseases. The sacrament must come first, they thought, and needful but slow instruction must come later. So Motolinía rebuked Las Casas when he refused to baptize a certain Indian: "How is this, Father, all this zeal and love that you say you have for the Indians is exhausted in loading them down and going around writing about Spaniards, and vexing the Indians"—encouraging them in rebellion?

Las Casas had insisted that the Indians were fully rational beings, not to be baptized *en masse* or without proper preparation, and he had won that point with Pope Paul III in *Sublimis Deus* (1537). The pope wrote to uphold natural human rights, to outlaw slavery, and to ameliorate abuses in the colonies. That encyclical, and the tireless efforts of Las Casas, had prevailed with Charles and the Spanish court, resulting in the so-called New Laws (1542), laws that horrified the Spanish settlers, because in their recognition of Indian rights they put in jeopardy the whole colonial world.

The conflict was not settled in a day. It could not be, given the vast distance between Spain and the colonies, the uncertainty of the reports reaching Spain, and the lack of means to enforce the royal will. The remarkable thing is that *there was such a conflict at all.* We find many an American advocate for Indian rights in the 19th century, and many an abolitionist inveighing against slavery from the comfort of a Massachusetts rectory. Bartolomé de las Casas preceded them by three hundred years, and he did more than write and talk.

Man of fire

The most influential of the works of Las Casas was his *Brief Account of the Destruction of the Indies* (1552), which concentrates in a nearly unbearable narrative his experiences among the Spanish settlers, along with much hearsay, hotly disputed by other Spaniards both lay and clerical. Here is a typically fiery passage:

"Thus the *Spaniards* blinded with the luster of their gold, deserted by God, and given over to a reprobate sense, not understanding (or at least not willing to do so) that the cause of the Indians is most just, as well by the law of Nature as the divine and human, then by force of arms destroying them, hacking them in pieces, and turning them out of their own confines and dominions, nor considering how unjust those violences and tyrannies are, wherewith they have afflicted these poor creatures, they still contrive to raise new Wars against them:

Nay they conceive, and by word and writing testify, that those victories they have obtained against those innocents to their ruin are granted them by God himself."

This work was popular among the English and Dutch colonialists, and formed the basis of the so-called Black Legend, still in force when Americans spoiled for war against Spain and her satellites in Mexico and Cuba.

But it's all to the credit of Spain that her best men and women did not dismiss Las Casas as a madman. They too wanted what he wanted, to fulfill the commission of Christ, to make disciples—not slaves, but disciples just as they were—of all nations. In this enterprise, as compromised by human sin as it sometimes is, they succeeded where other conquerors never bothered to try. An uneasy conscience is far better than none.

The Delicate Nest

"And this Catholic Church," wrote the scholar and priest, "so weak in herself, so strong in her God, what a spectacle her history presents! Only now we behold her, in the very infancy of her existence, tossed by persecution, and almost drowned in blood; but God, who enables the reed to stand before the gale that uproots the oak of centuries—God, whose providence sustains the sea-bird's delicate nest on the foaming wave..."—and he puts down his pen and does not finish the sentence.

"A delicate nest," he says, and his mind returns to a sunny day in September, on the shores of the ocean. He and his beloved wife Louisa had gone to the resort town of Torquay. Cholera had ravaged the land. That morning he went to Mass, and when he came back, Louisa was ill. She died that night. She was only twenty-eight years old.

He knew what his brother would think. It was a judgment against him. For he had enjoyed a good living as an Anglican curate, in the diocese of his uncle the bishop, and he gave that all up when he and Louisa had left the English church to commit themselves to the Church of Rome.

"You are seeking to destroy our happy home," said Alfred.

"I must follow my conscience in this matter."

"You are not following your conscience. You are following that self-important knave, Dr. Newman."

"He too must follow where the truth leads."

"Truth?" said Alfred. "You break your faith, and you pledge yourself to a foreign church, and be assured, that church is doomed. What truth are you talking about?"

Edward Caswall, priest and poet, translator and composer of hymns, knew what truth it was, and tried to see God's hand in that day long ago on the coast. Louisa had seen it, if Alfred could not. And he took up his pen again.

In the light of the eternal

Father Caswall was not a great scientist, like the monk Gregor Mendel. He did not rule a nation, like Saint Louis IX of France. He did not found a missionary order, like Saint Ignatius of Loyola. He did not paint the Sistine Chapel, or write the greatest plays in the history of the world.

Yet we ought to see his life as somehow of his age, Victorian England, and not of his age; a man formed by the faith and its history, but whose work, gentle, pious, and touching all features of Christian worship, was the leaven in the dough for his time, and will last as long as English is spoken; the standard-setter for English hymnody, whose greatest influence I am persuaded is yet to come.

After Louisa Caswall died in 1849, Edward determined to seek holy orders as a Catholic priest. He joined the Birmingham Oratory (founded by Newman), where he lived until his death in 1878, and was ordained a priest in 1852. The Cardinal was the superior at the Oratory, but he was often absent, and to Caswall would fall the duties of his friend, in addition to his regular oversight of the Oratory's finances.

But we do not know Edward Caswall for his practical skills as a manager. We know him—or we ought to know him—for his hymns.

The Church has her daily office, her prayer-duty, for the eight canonical hours of the day, and for all the seasons and feasts of the year. Each hour, each day, each season, each feast has its song: and so Caswall, classically educated, set himself the task of translating every single one of them into English poetry, more than four hundred pages of hymnody. Here is a stanza from the first, for matins for Sunday:

So, while on this his holy day,
At this most sacred hour,
Our psalms amid the stillness rise,
May he his blessings shower.

Simplicity and clarity were Caswall's strengths, and it is always easy to underestimate them. But in his words we find an awareness that there is always more to the world than we see before us: more beauty, a deeper mystery, and the light of eternity shining quietly upon and through the works of time. Here the priest regards the sea, and remembers his boyhood, and considers the world to come:

The thoughts which my childhood beguiled
Were an emblem, I well perceive how;
As I thought of the sea when a child,
So I think of eternity now.
I stand by the side of its sea,
I gather the shells on its shore;
But its depths are mysterious to me
As the depths of the ocean of yore.

Ever the child

Cardinal Newman once humorously said of his old friend Caswall that he was "half a saint." Saint or not, he was always more than half a child. Sometimes he had the harmless mischief of a child. Here's how the young Caswall began his "Sketches of Young Ladies," which were published along with "Sketches of Young Gentlemen" by Charles Dickens. "We have often regretted," he says, "that while so much genius has of late years been employed in classification of the vegetable and animal kingdom, the classification of young ladies has been totally and unaccountably neglected." For example, there is the Young Lady Who Sings. You'll meet her at a party, and after she drops a hint about Italian food, she will ask you if you are fond of music. "Beware of answering in the affirmative," says Caswall.

His admiration of the fair sex was deep, though, as was his devotion to Mary and to the humanity of Jesus, and that should guarantee that his hymns will be a pattern for authors and composers to come. Look at the first stanza of his lovely Christmas carol:

Sleep, holy babe,
Upon thy mother's breast!
Great Lord of earth and sea and sky,
How sweet it is to see thee lie
In such a place of rest.

Caswall places himself and us there at the manger too:

Sleep, holy babe,
While I with Mary gaze
In joy upon that face awhile,
Upon the loving infant smile
That there divinely plays.

But it is no mere sentimentality. Father Caswall knew, as his countryman Dickens knew, that the Father reveals the Son not to the high and mighty, but to innocents and fools, to those who press upon the gates of heaven like eager children. So we have his fine doxology at the end of a hymn for the Transfiguration:

To Jesus, from the proud concealed,
But evermore to babes revealed,
All glory with the Father be,
And Holy Ghost, eternally.

It is the child's longing in love.

Tenderness amid the smoke

We hear that we have to tailor the message of Jesus to the audience, but we should never suppose that ordinary people aren't capable of appreciating real beauty, just because they live in a bustling, grimy, ugly industrial city like Birmingham, and were not educated at Oxford, as Father Caswall was. Notice the mingling of tenderness, clear vision, and intellectual strength in his description of the school in Birmingham that he and Newman and he had founded, staffed by women who volunteered their services. "The unusual sight has been seen," he wrote, "of between thirty and forty boys entirely obedient to the firm but gentle control of a lady's hand." In later years, he said, these children, both boys and girls, would come to treasure the inestimable advantage they had been given, of being brought into contact "with the minds of persons belonging to a sphere above their own."

Is not that what sacred song and poetry should do? Not raise a yawn or a roll of the eyes, but bring us, children as we are, into a spiritual and intellectual sphere far beyond that of the ordinary day? Think of this famous medieval hymn, sweetly translated into English by Father Caswall:

Jesu! the very thought of thee
With sweetness fills my breast,
But sweeter far thy face to see,
And in thy presence rest.

Father Caswall left the world among us gently too. Cardinal Newman would write these words to the priest's sister: "He seems to have felt that he was drawing to his end, for in the middle of the day he began to express his sense of God's mercies in having been so tender and careful of him all through his life, and having kept him from pain during his last illness. He was one of my dearest friends, and is a great loss to us all, for he was loved far and wide round about the Oratory."

I find no fitter way to end than with a few stanzas from a gentle hymn for the close of the day, preparing for the evening of life:

The sun is sinking fast,
The daylight dies;
Let love awake, and pay
Her evening sacrifice.
As Christ upon the cross
His head inclined,
And to his Father's hands

His parting soul resigned,
So now herself my soul
Would wholly give
Into his sacred charge,
In whom all spirits live.

"Into your hands, O Lord, I commend my spirit," said the Lord. We must say so too. Father Caswall has given us the means even to sing it.

A Folk Song for the Lord

It's Christmas Eve, 1818, in the Austrian village of Oberndorf bei Salzburg. The organist and choirmaster for the parish church is resting a little before the most strenuous work of the holy season. The house is still. Herr Gruber and his wife have had two children, but they rest beneath the earth of the churchyard.

A knock at the door. *"Grüss Gott!"* says the organist, giving his visitor the traditional Austrian hello. "Joseph, did you walk all the way here? Is there something wrong?"

"Grüss Gott!" says his friend, a young Catholic priest. He has in fact walked the three miles to his friend's house, and he has never had a strong constitution. "Franz, I'm here to ask you a favor. On Christmas Eve, no less." "Anything you wish," says Franz, with some hesitation as he glances to the clock.

"I have a poem here that I wrote two years ago, on the birth of Jesus," says Father Joseph, and he hands a sheet of paper to the organist, who reads it silently. "Why, this is lovely, Joseph. Maria," he calls to his wife, "come and see the poem that Father has written." Maria, mother no longer, or mother forever, reads the poem as she stands by her husband's shoulder. "So beautiful," she says. "Franz, you should do what Father wants. You'll have time. I'll save your supper for later, and Father, you must join us."

"Can you write the music for me, Franz? I will play the melody on my guitar. Think of it as a folk song."

"Yes, an Austrian song," says Franz, and he sits down at the clavier.

Stille Nacht, Heilige Nacht

You must imagine all the solemnity and the glory of the Christmas High Mass at midnight, the many candles casting their warm soft light throughout the church, while the snow outside shines softly under the wintry moon. Imagine the priests and the long train of altar boys, and the people in the pews, a few of them well-to-do, most of them ordinary laborers and their wives and children, dressed in their holiday clothes. They will be the first to hear a song that billions of people will hear.

The Mass is ended; the Last Gospel is said. Then Father Joseph Mohr and the choir of the church of Saint Nicholas gather in front of the Nativity. They don't have the music to the song, because there wasn't time to make any copies. That doesn't matter. They're quick to learn. Father Mohr begins, picking out the melody we know, and he sings the first of six stanzas:

Stille Nacht, heilige Nacht!
Alles schläft, einsam wacht
Nur das traute hochheilige Paar.
Holder Knabe im lockigen Haar,
Schlaf in himmlischer Ruh,
Schlaf in himmlischer Ruh!

Whose meaning I'll give here word for word:

Silent night, holy night!
All are sleeping; they alone are awake,
The wedded and most holy pair.
Gentle child with curly hair,
Sleep in heavenly peace,
Sleep in heavenly peace!

The choir sings the last two lines of every verse in four-part harmony. It's the carol we know and love, perhaps the sweetest of all carols, from that part of the Catholic world where the tenderest love was showered upon the Christ Child. Let me give here two of the stanzas that we probably don't know, again with the English meaning:

Stille Nacht, heilige Nacht,
Die der Welt Heil gebracht,
Aus des Himmels goldenen Höhn,
Uns der Gnaden Fülle läßt sehn,
Jesum in Menschengestalt,
Jesum in Menschengestalt!

Stille Nacht, heilige Nacht,
Wo sich heut alle Macht
Väterlicher Liebe ergoß,
Und als Bruder huldvoll umschloß
Jesus die Völker der Welt,
Jesus die Völker der Welt!

Silent night, holy night,
That has brought the salvation of the world,
Giving us to behold the fullness of grace
From the golden heights of heaven—
Jesus, in the form of man,
Jesus, in the form of man!

Silent night, holy night,
On which the whole power
Of fatherly love pours itself forth,
And Jesus as our brother graciously embraces
All the peoples of the world,
All the peoples of the world!

You see, it's not just for Austria. The miracle of Christmas is that our Lord and Maker has come to dwell among us as man among men. He, and not some Kaiser or politician or warlord, brings us *Heil:* makes us *whole,* brings *salvation.* It was fitting that Father Mohr wrote that poem, because in his own life the light had broken forth from darkness.

From an unlikely place

"Jo," says the mother, draping her needlework over the arm of a threadbare chair, "fetch the good Father the tea from the kitchen, and bring the loaf of bread with some butter." She gets up uneasily and offers the priest a seat. While the boy is gone, the priest says softly, "Fraulein Anna, your son is a clever lad." At the word *Fraulein* she glances to the floor and toward the kitchen. "What do people like us have to do with cleverness?" she says.

"It is a gift from God," says the priest. He knows what troubles her. "Where is Joseph's father?"

"He may be dead for all we know."

"Many a soldier leads a wayward life," says the priest.

"He was not even a good soldier," says she. "A runaway."

"And he ran from you and the boy also?"

"He ran away before the boy was even born." "It was you, then, who named him Joseph." "Yes, Joseph. He knew how to protect a mother and her son."

The boy comes back with a big tray, heaped with bread, a jar of elderberry jam, fresh butter, and a steaming pot of tea. His face is flushed with excitement.

"I want to send Joseph to school," the priest declares. The woman hesitates. Such a blessing—but how can it be?

"My son has no right father."

"He has a Father in heaven."

"But to be a priest," she says, almost as if arguing against it, for a priest must have been born within wedlock. "We will see to that when the time comes," says the priest, and then he turns to Joseph. The boy is thin and somewhat weak. Not the fullest meals, apparently. "Joseph, I wish to send you to the cathedral school in Salzburg. Would you like to come? We will take care of your mother."

"Yes, Father—I've been praying for that."

A poor child always

Joseph Mohr went to that school, where he became known as a brilliant student. He played the violin and sang in the cathedral choir, and at age sixteen went away to study philosophy with the Benedictines. At eighteen he returned to Salzburg, and one year later entered the seminary. He had to obtain a special dispensation for that, and also to be ordained a priest at the early age of twenty-two. Wherever he went, Father Mohr brought with him his learning, his love for music, and his care for the poor. When he died he had nothing to his name, because he had given it all away, all except for his violin. His last assignment was to be the pastor of Wagrain, a village in the Austrian Alps. He led the choir there too and composed sacred music for it to sing. Right away he built a school for the village children, a school that was later named for its beloved founder. He built also a home for the poor and the sick.

For it troubled him deeply that the custom there in the Alps was that the poor would travel from one house to the next, staying at each for a couple of days, where they would be given food and shelter, but then they would have to move on. That sounds generous and humane, and it surely was more personal than the care that we Americans give to our poor, but you can imagine what it must have been like in the winter, when such people had to fight the wind and the cold and the deep snow, and sometimes they did not survive it. You must also imagine Father Mohr himself, traveling from one house to another to serve his flock in all kinds of weather. He died in December of 1848, at the young age of fifty-five.

Christ the Savior is born!

Some people say that Father Mohr did not live to see how cherished his song would be, but that's not so. Already in 1839 it was performed at a church halfway across the world, in New York City. It was regularly sung by Austrian and German choirs. It is true that for many years nobody knew who had composed the simple and lovely melody. Some people attributed it to Mozart or Beethoven.

But we know that it was Father Mohr's friend. One copy in Mohr's hand survives. It reads, simply, *Weihnachts-lied—Christmas Song.* On the right at the top, Mohr has written the words *Melodie von Fr. Xav. Gruber.* The two men remained the closest of friends all their lives, and they continued to work together on sacred music.

Silent Night is probably the one Christmas carol that everyone knows, even people who do not know Jesus. Let us pray that someday it will bring even those poor souls to the crèche or the throne of our Lord. For it is as the final words of the poem read, in Father Mohr's elegant hand: *Jesus der Retter ist da! Jesus der Retter ist da!* Jesus the Savior is here!

God Makes No Mistakes

The year is 1013, and we are in the castle of the Count of Altshausen, in Swabia. The countess lies in her bed, weeping freely. In her arms she cradles a newborn lump of humanity covered with blood, a boy child. His face seems jolted out of shape, and his body—it is a body, somehow. "You are so pitiful," she cries, "my poor little boy."

The count looks on. "Fetch the priest," he says to one of his servants. And the thought passes through his mind that it might be a mercy if the child died after he had been baptized. He fights the thought with prayer.

"My dear," he says, "we will give this child to God. He will do what is best."

The priest comes, and they christen the boy Hermann, "fighting man" in the old German tongue. He will be one of fifteen children, and Werner, one of his brothers, will indeed be a fighter at the side of Hildebrand, the great reforming Pope Gregory VII.

Carried to school for life

It is 1020. The boy can hardly grunt out his words, though his mind is sharp as any sword. He cannot move even a few feet without help. He must be carried or wheeled about. People will give him the nickname *Contractus*, or "doubled over."

The count and countess have taken the boy to the island of Reichenau, in Lake Constance, to meet Berno, the saintly abbot of the monastery there.

"Our Hermann cannot read or write, my lord," says the count, "but he can see things I can't, and he can explain the Latin of the Mass to me, and he can make great reckonings by searching for them, like this. Watch. Hermann," he says to the boy, laying his hand on his head, "Our good lord the abbot has forty-three sheep he wishes to sell at twenty-nine silver pieces a head. How many..."—but before he finishes the boy twists his head to one side, looking up, and groans happily.

"What does he say?"

"One thousand two hundred forty-seven. Is that right?"

"I'll see," says the abbot, scratching upon a scrap of parchment. They don't yet have Arabic numerals in those days, so the calculation is cumbersome. "Remarkable," says the abbot. "Hermann," he says to the boy, "do you wish to live with us here, and serve God? I will teach you all I know."

"Yes!" the boy cries, with a contraction of his muscles.

And so Hermann the Cripple came to the place where he would live many years full of intellectual and spiritual work, for the rest of his life.

The music of heaven

"The earth is a globe, as you know," says the hunchback in the chair, moving a slide along the side of a cylinder covered with a variety of curved lines. A group of young men gathers about. They have come from far away, so they and their teacher speak in Latin, the language they all know. He could speak to them in Hebrew, but they would not know what he was saying.

"The sun travels around our globe, but where? That depends on how far north you are from the celestial equator, and what day of the year it is," he says, and he goes on to explain to the young men how the path of the sun makes a spiral across the sky from the spring balance of equal day and night to its summer standstill, whereupon it reverses direction.

The men knit their brows, and one of them says, "Master, it's the eleventh of May. Show us the path." At which Hermann smiles and moves the slide.

"See," says Hermann, "the sun at noon today will be at sixty degrees from the horizon here at Reichenau," and he explains why. "If you take the sundial out, you will see the shadow reach to this point," which he indicates with a crooked finger.

"The shadow will be short, Master," and Hermann answers his pupil's question before he asks it. "Yes," says Hermann. "It will be the third part of the root of three."

"Master," says the lad, "this machine you call the *astrolabe* is a wonderful thing. It's as if it played silent music."

"Numbers are silent music, and music is number for the ear," says Hermann, and then the bells toll the hour of Prime. The monks leave for the chapel, with one of them wheeling Hermann along.

Orders of mind and deed

Hermann the Cripple was a polymath who attracted scholars from far and near. He wrote two treatises on the astrolabe; they were the first such in Europe. He made his own astronomical devices, too. He wrote a long treatise on the mathematics of the eight musical modes, describing their harmonies according to precise ratios. You'd better get out your calculator to read it. He invented a variety of musical instruments.

Why should a monk do that? Why not? Hermann saw himself in that long tradition coming from the mystic and mathematician Pythagoras, through the philosophers and the Church Fathers to Boethius, another polymath who wrote about everything under the sun, including music. Hermann does not seem to have been aware that Guido of Arezzo, whose life overlapped with his, developed a system of musical notation. Hermann invented his own. He wrote a chronicle of important events occurring each year from the time of Christ to his own day, subsequently continued by his best student, Berthold.

He probably suffered from a cleft palate and cerebral palsy, though some suggest that it was a slowly degenerative form of Lou Gehrig's disease. By all accounts he had a sunny personality, and he often joked about his ugly and ungainly body. He was called *hilarissimus*—cheery, we might put it. People sometimes say that when you cannot enjoy what ordinary people do, you become sour and resentful. With Hermann it was the other way around. Because he could not enjoy those ordinary things, he did not take himself too seriously, nor did he miss the pleasures of this world. "If things don't suffice for you," he quipped, "make yourself sufficient for things, and you'll be all the greater for not desiring more than you have."

He kept *in order* what was good. You can see it in a wonderful poem he wrote at the request of a convent of sisters to whom he ministered. They were his "little sisters," very dear to him, and he was their "Herimannulus," their Little Hermann. He begins by begging his friend the Muse to sing something that would delight the sisters, mingling the comical with the serious, as was the habit in the Middle Ages. We have only the first book, 1,720 lines long, written in a staggering variety of meters, with Hermann, the Sisters, and the Muse Melpomene all having their speaking parts. It's a delightful foray into the vanity of worldly desires, with Melpomene devoting quite a while to *eight deadly vices*—yes, eight: pride, followed by vainglory, envy, wrath, sadness, avarice, gluttony, and lust.

Notice the one in the middle: *tristitia,* sadness. We call it sloth now, but it has to do with sluggishness of soul, a failure to delight in what should delight us. It all begins, Hermann says, with our care for *caducis nugulis,* foolish little things that fall away. That leads to care, anxiety, weariness, strife, sorrow, and madness, and causes us to sin unto death against God. Hermann himself did not worry about what others had and he did not. When his beloved teacher Berno died in 1048, the monks of Reichenau made Hermann the Cripple their abbot. It is a fine testimony to what they thought of his misshapen body and his fine and robust soul.

And he too shall sing

"Hermann," he identifies himself in one of his works on the astrolabe, "the rubbish of Christ's poor ones, among the recruits of philosophy slower than a donkey or a snail." Donkeys and snails don't sing, nor could Hermann, not with his voice anyway. But he not only wrote about music. He composed it, too. Two of the hymns often attributed to him have come to be loved throughout the Catholic world, the *Alma Redemptoris Mater* and the *Salve Regina.* Yes, whenever you say the last prayer of your rosary, remember that it was composed by the little man who could not walk, the lover of music who could not sing. It's possible also that he is the author of *Veni Sancte Spiritus:* "Come, Holy Ghost."

Had Hermann been born in pagan times, they would have given him back to the gods or the wild beasts by exposing him on a hillside. We are even less pious now. He might not have been born. Let us thank God that Hermann lived at the bright dawn of the high Middle Ages, and that his mother and father were good Christians, and that the abbot Berno understood that the gifts of God come in ways the world will not see. Consider that Blessed Hermann now stands upright in the presence of God, and that when the saints sing of the glory of our Savior who was born in poverty, his voice will keep pace with the racing of his heart, nor will it sound like the braying of a donkey. May we someday sing as well!

Sculpting the Breath of God

"Sometimes when I come to visit you, my boy," said the cardinal, immensely pleased as he paced about the workshop, "I think that God has struck us for our sins and reduced the world to its original chaos." For there were strewn about the room blocks of stone, rubble, marble dust, lumps of wet clay, straw for the clay, great *cartoni* scrawled over with sketches, files, chisels, hammers, and paint, a head of an angel here, a half of a wing there, and a street lad for a model. Today the model was sitting cross-legged on the floor, munching at a hunk of bread and some cheese. "Gian Lorenzo, can't you ever sculpt anything *at rest*?" the cardinal said.

"God is always in action, and so am I," said the young sculptor. He'd been in action since he was a boy prodigy.

"I wonder," said the cardinal, "have you ever been to Florence?" "No, I have not," said the sculptor, moving about an enormous marble block, eyeing it from this angle and that. "No, I have not seen what Michelangelo did with David. I know it from drawings."

"I can take you to Florence to see it."

"No, my lord," said the lad, pausing in his work. His brow gleamed with sweat. "No, I don't think so. No one can match him at the kind of thing he did. I must do something else."

"They say that he sculpted the fire of David's soul. What will you sculpt?"

"I will sculpt his action," said Gian Lorenzo Bernini. "Action. And air. I will sculpt air."

Cardinal Borghese broke out into a hearty laugh. "No man can sculpt air," he said. "But if any man could, it would be you."

An art of energy

Bernini did just that. You can go to the Villa Borghese in Rome and see his sculpture of David, which is nothing like Michelangelo's colossus or Donatello's naked boy poised like a Greek cupid over Goliath's severed head. It's a young man in the midst of violent action, bent over, body ready to uncoil, his sling extended from one arm to the other, his lips bitten in that unwitting way we have when we are straining with all our might. Yet you do not get the impression of heaviness or difficulty. That is because David's balance is perfect. And what you notice first is the air—yes, the air, blowing his hair back from his head, in the swift breeze caused by his own motion.

That is Baroque art for you, so much of it inspired by the Catholic Reformation and its immense energy. That movement sent missionaries to every corner of the world: think of Saint Francis Xavier.

It produced literature of extraordinary range and depth: think of Cervantes and *Don Quixote*. It inspired wholly new forms of music: think of Saint Philip Neri and the oratorio. In Gian Lorenzo Bernini, it had a sculptor who seemed to revel in trying to do in stone what you would think gravity itself could not allow.

Go to his Fountain of the Four Rivers, in the Piazza Navona, in Rome. The allegorical rivers, represented by four colossal nudes, come forth from what looks like four angles of a cliff, except—the cliff has no interior! It is all open inside, wide enough for a horse to be seen coming through. Atop the cliff stands an ancient Roman copy of an Egyptian obelisk, eighty feet tall, and resting on—what? On air, it appears; it is as if the obelisk hangs from the sky.

That fountain was built to honor the Church and the authority of the successor to Saint Peter. Jesus commanded his disciples to go forth and preach to all nations, baptizing them in the name of the Father, the Son, and the Holy Spirit. The Church in Bernini's time was doing just that, going to lands that no one had known about before. The rivers in the fountain are the Danube, for Europe; but also the Ganges, for Asia, the Nile, for Africa, and the La Plata, for the Americas.

The chair of Peter

So it shouldn't surprise us to find that the celebrated Bernini, the artistic master of Rome, should be called upon by Pope Alexander VII to elevate a relic of the chair of Saint Peter to the prominence it deserved.

It was an old oaken chair, riddled by age, and supplemented over the centuries with metal rings and fasteners, and wooden additions. Its inner skeleton of acacia might indeed have come from the earliest years of the Church. Tradition has it that Saint Peter presided in Rome from the original chair. It would be displayed every year during Holy Week, along with the veronica, the cloth with which the holy woman wiped the face of Jesus. But Alexander wanted it to be shown at all times. So the first thing Bernini did was to fashion a bronze chair to enclose it, bronze laid over with gold. Yes, the chair of wood is the interior now of a chair of bronze. You might say that it shows the mortal enfolded by the immortal. Its "upholstery," that is, the bronze relief sculpture that in a wooden chair would be the cloth covering the back, shows Jesus giving the keys of the kingdom to Saint Peter.

That is well and good, but where do you *put* this chair? Think of it for a moment. It is no ordinary chair. It is the site of the action of God, because only God can raise up a mere man to become the vicar of Christ upon earth. Where should the chair go?

Between heaven and earth

Bernini's solution is breathtaking. When you go to Saint Peter's and you look through and beyond his magnificent bronze *baldacchino,* the canopy upon spiraling pillars that stands over the altar, you will see the chair, but how it can be where it is, that is the wonder of it. It appears to be coming forth from the wall of the basilica itself, in clouds of glory, with angels roundabout and long golden rays like an explosion of light. Beneath it stand four figures, fifteen feet high: Saint Ambrose and Saint Athanasius on the left, and Saint Augustine and Saint John Chrysostom on the right. The figures in front, Ambrose and Augustine, wear the bishop's miter. They are from the west, while Athanasius and John are from the east. The pope thus presides for the whole of the Christian people.

You might think that these Fathers of the ancient Church are holding up Peter's chair, but it isn't exactly so. They touch it, with their palms down, as if they were lifting something as light as a feather. I've heard someone say that it looks for all the world as if they were restraining the chair, lightly—but I think that the power is all in the chair, flowing from it into them.

I still have not mentioned the most marvelous thing of all. The great pillars and walls of Saint Peter's suggest tremendous might and weight. But what about the action of the Holy Spirit, which is like the wind that blows where it will? For the man who sits in the see of Peter is made Bishop of Rome and vicar of Christ by that same Spirit. How do you sculpt breath?

This is what Bernini did. He pierced the back wall with a window of alabaster, lightly colored in white and gold-red and gold, with the Holy Spirit as a dove in its center, its wings extended in flight. From the dove come forth rays, divided into twelve sections, for the twelve apostles, and each of those twelve divided in turn into six, for the seventy-two disciples whom Jesus commissioned to preach and to heal in his name. This is not so much a skylight as a dove-light, a Spirit-light; and when the sun shines through it, it seems like a window into heaven, the only such window on earth.

The permanent things

Bernini, the boy genius, died of a stroke in 1680, at the good old age of eighty-one. He was working till the end. For a long time, classical critics did not hold him in high repute. The Baroque was too passionate for their cold palates. But now Bernini is recognized as a truly unique artist, as great in his way as Michelangelo was in his, and for sheer technical virtuosity—see the laurel leaves sprouting from the fingers of the girl in mid-metamorphosis in his *Apollo and Daphne*—no one has been his equal.

We honor the man and his work, but we know, as he himself did, that the Chair of Peter is of a higher reality altogether. Catholics celebrate the feast of the Chair of Peter on February 22. Heaven and earth may pass away, and with them all the works of man, but the promise of Christ does not pass away. To Peter he gave the keys to the kingdom, as it was his prerogative to do. That promise he has not revoked. "For behold," he says, "I am with you always, to the end of time."

There Will Your Heart Be Also

Indulge me, reader, while I set a remarkable stage.

In 1837, Francis Martin Drexel, a Catholic émigré from Austria, a portrait painter, founded a banking house in Philadelphia. He painted the rich, so he had come to know who among them was morally solid and who was not. He brought his oldest sons, Francis and Anthony, into the business. They were thirteen and eleven years old. When the gold rush struck in California in 1849, the elder Drexel set up shop there, while the lads ran the business back home. The Drexel bank became one of the richest in the nation, helping to finance the Union Army during the Civil War.

In 1860, the son Francis, a young widower with two daughters, Elizabeth and Katharine ("Katie" as they called her), married a woman named Emma Bouvier. Emma brought him more deeply into his Catholic faith. He would come home from work and retire to play sacred music on the organ; and he and Emma and the girls—a third daughter was born to them—set aside time every evening to pray and sing in the room she set up as an oratory.

Prayer and song were not their only expressions of faith. Acts of the heart accompanied them.

Throughout the week, Emma's agent, Mary Bilger, visited the slums in Philadelphia, looking for people in need: widows and orphans; people, white and colored, displaced from devastated lands in the south; the human sawdust of the industrial revolution. She gave them tickets to show up at the Drexel house. There Emma spoke to them face to face, with the girls present. Mostly they needed money for rent, groceries, and clothing—especially shoes. This was *personal* charity. Emma had a stake in the success of those to whom she gave. She kept records. She told the girls it was wrong to cast money broadside. You must have, she wrote, "the keenness of a knave, the kindness of a fool, and the judgment of a philosopher."

The wealth she gave yearly, with her husband's glad approval, was immense. But she gave more from her person. Katie inherited from her parents a vibrant and active faith; determination to get jobs done; the shrewdness of a businessman; and humility—the humility to be involved in the lives of the lowliest of men.

Go west, young woman

It is 1887. Francis and Emma have passed away. The Drexel girls, "We Three" as they jestingly call themselves, are in Rome. It's been a long journey. They are wealthy heiresses, seeking to do God's work. They have visited many a monastery, begging for priests and sisters to come to the western world to minister to the Indians. Now they stand before Pope Leo XIII.

"Why not, my child," said the pope to Katharine, "yourself become a missionary?"

Why the Indians? In 1881, the editors of *The Century Magazine,* Protestants not unfriendly to the Catholic Church, sent Helen Hunt Jackson out west to write about the state of the Indian tribes. She visited the California missions, in ruins since the Mexican War. She pored over the records the friars kept. She spoke to old people who remembered the time of the fathers, rich times, when there was plenty to eat, when thousands of Indians in the missions became farmers, herders, weavers, millers, vintners, blacksmiths, tanners, and engineers. "Dem work for civilize," said an elderly Indian to her, "not for money. Dey work to religion."

Imagine the contrast between the coasts: on the Atlantic, "the descendants of the Puritans, weighed down by serious purpose, half grudging the time for their one staid yearly Thanksgiving, and driving the Indians farther and farther into the wilderness every year," killing them while they were at it, while on the Pacific, "the merry people of Mexican and Spanish blood...dancing away whole days and nights like children, while their priests were gathering the Indians by thousands into communities, and feeding and teaching them."

That was gone, and Americans were much to blame. Jackson's book, *A Century of Dishonor*, describing a hundred years of neglect, error, and treachery, kindled a fire in Katie's soul. She too went west in 1884 and toured the country, meeting the Dakota wise man Red Cloud, who pleaded with her to send the "black robes" there to teach his people. Jackson, "Helen of Colorado" as Emily Dickinson called her, was dying of stomach cancer. I like to think that Katie sought her out in her journey. What had been done before could be done again. The Church must do it.

The least of these

It is 1893, and Katie, now Mother Katharine Mary Drexel of the new Sisters of the Blessed Sacrament for Indians and Colored People, is writing to her small flock. She has given up the social life of a Philadelphia heiress. It took her years to persuade her old parish priest and spiritual director, Father James O'Connor, now Bishop of Omaha, that she had a vocation to the religious life. She has appealed to Patrick Ryan, Archbishop of Philadelphia, for permission to set out among the Indians. He refuses. Her order is too young, too new. They must wait.

"Sisters," she says, "we can make an act of humility, we are not fit instruments for apostolic labor among the Indians of New Mexico. Do not let this, however, deter us in the work of our sanctification." You can't give what you don't have. Mother Katharine had money. That was not enough. Money is only instrumental. The sisters wanted to give to blacks and Indians a share in the life of God. Hence, she says, they must die to themselves and let God reign in their hearts, and then "he will in his own time choose us to go and work in his vineyard," to bring in the bountiful harvest of souls.

See the ledger of Saint Katharine Drexel's apostolate: intelligence, determination, and a loving humility. When Archbishop Ryan finally agreed that her order was ready, she was a dynamo in action. Klansmen burnt a cross on the grounds of her motherhouse. But what was a little fire and wood, against the factory of love burning in her heart? Some people thought she had fled to the convent in sorrow. That was nonsense, she said. "I am, and I have always been, one of the happiest women in the world."

The Sisters built schools everywhere, from the tidewater of Virginia to the California coast. I'm looking at a photo of Mother Katharine among several small black children dressed in white, in front of a school. She's leaning over, holding the littlest, who seems to have lost something in the grass. Another photo: she is standing by the wall of a churchyard with several Indians, most of them elderly, with years of poverty, suffering, and endurance carved into their faces. She extends her right hand to touch the right hand of an old man. Another: she's bent over, smiling, her face tanned from the southern sun, as she pins a flower to the coat of a little Indian girl, perhaps for her first Communion.

The greatest of her projects, twenty years in the making, was a college for black people, the only such Catholic college in the country: Xavier University in New Orleans. I see a photo of Mother Katharine in a kitchen there, with pans on the stove, and seven young black women roundabout her—listening to a recipe for soup, it seems! Surely she kept the vows she had made so long before, promising poverty, chastity, and obedience, in an effort "to be the Mother and Servant of the Indian and Negro races," and never to undertake any work which might tend to their neglect or abandonment.

May the sun rise again

That Katie who knew President Grant as a family friend, who petitioned President Hayes on behalf of the Dakotas, lived to see a distant cousin on her mother's side, Jacqueline, marry a man named John, soon to be president. Through all her ninety-six years, she used her father's fortune in wise and generous ways, though she herself lived plainly and simply. "Desire little in this world," she advised her sisters. Rather they should resign themselves to "the loving Providence of God [their] Father." She might well think of the prudence and generosity and diligence of her father and mother, who built a house of sanctity, as did the Martin family in France for their beloved Thérèse.

It's easy in our time to have the still, small voice of conscience drowned out by the noise of political action and enmity. We should then ask why Mother Katharine devoted her sisters and her order to the Blessed Sacrament. Jesus is present there, really, fully, not just as a sign. Mother Katharine did not choose to help the Indians and blacks from the haven of political signs. She lived with them. She rode burros beside them. She fed them and housed them. She prayed with them. She was small with them. In Christ, she was great with them.

May the sun of her charism rise among us again.

Stronger than Steel

The sergeant stood before the young soldier in the cold rain. Some men shuffled about them. Most were smirking. A few hung their heads.

"Beads are for girls," said the sergeant, "or worse. That's what you are, isn't it?"

The soldier shut his eyes and did not reply.

"Look here," said the sergeant, with mocking friendliness. He flung the soldier's rosary to the ground. "Wood is wood. Nothing else. Tread on those beads. Show that you're a man and not a girl. Now!"

"Sir, I will not."

"Afraid your mama will strike you dead from the sky?" The sergeant called out another private from the men nearby, a city boy who believed in nothing. "You, tread this thing into the mud."

The boy did.

"No lightning, Popiełuszko. No lightning. But who knows? Maybe it will come. Why don't you stand at attention here to wait for the lightning? At attention!"

And he left him there. Alphons Popiełuszko was accustomed to such treatment. The Polish communists sent seminarians into the army to indoctrinate them or shame them out of their vocations.

The beatings, the privations, the humiliations—all because he was a Catholic and a Pole and not a secular toady for the Soviet lords and their Polish co-operators—ruined his health for the rest of his life.

The seed in the dark earth

The young man returned to the vocation he had discerned when he was a boy. He was ordained in 1972, at age twenty-four. He took the name Jerzy, the Polish name we know as George. That was fitting, for two reasons. One is that the name means *a tiller of the earth*. Father Popiełuszko grew up on a farm in the village of Okopy, on the western bank of the Bug River, the border between Poland and modern-day Ukraine. Such a place was as the plains of Kansas are to the cultural elites in New York City: good for grain, and otherwise to ignore. The other reason is Saint George himself, patron of soldiers. The boy Alphons saw through the swagger of the communists in the Polish army. The man George—Father Jerzy—would become, not by his own design but by the providence of God working through his fidelity, a great warrior for truth and against the lies of the communist regime.

Think of those dark years. The Soviet Union seemed as immovable as the continents it spanned. The United States would soon withdraw from the fight against the communists in Vietnam. No one suspected that there would soon be a Polish pope, or that *workers themselves* would unite in Poland to protest the supposed workman's paradise. The wisdom of the world was blind.

No one suspected the role that Father Jerzy would play in the coming drama of freedom, perhaps he least of all. He was a priest in Warsaw, where he would eventually serve at the parish of Saint Stanislaus Kostka. That too was fitting. Stanislaus was a boy saint, remarkable for his piety. His own older brother Paul, in exasperation, would insult and beat him, but Stanislaus endured it with patience, finally fleeing to enter a Jesuit seminary, dying at age eighteen, on the feast of the Assumption. Father Jerzy was the man that Stanislaus might have been, physically frail but fearless, a sensitive soul who ministered to men as hard as the steel they wrought.

For that is what happened: Father Jerzy was assigned to be the chaplain to steelworkers in Warsaw. He learned to do the heavy jobs they did, sweating beside them. He urged them never to capitulate to a lie. And more: "It is not enough," he said, "for a Christian to condemn evil, cowardice, lies, and use of force, hatred, and oppression. He must at all times be a witness to and defender of justice, goodness, truth, freedom, and love." His preaching began to draw large crowds. His words were broadcast over Radio Free Europe, that shaft of light sent through the fissures in the Iron Curtain.

Then came Solidarity, and John Paul II, and the brave electrician Lech Wałęsa.

War and peace

Late in 1981, the Polish communists declared a state of martial law, and outlawed Solidarity—with its nine million members. By this time, Father Jerzy was the spiritual leader of the movement. The workers did not go to the Church authorities, who had worked out a *modus vivendi* with the communists and did not want trouble. American diplomats, strangely deaf to the calls of the spirit, could see only that the Polish regime didn't kill a lot of people. Why, some party members might even attend Mass.

Father Jerzy came to the United States that year to attend his aunt's funeral, and he could have stayed; General Jaruszelski, the head of state, would have preferred it. But Father Jerzy said of the workers, "They need me and I need them."

His activity over the next three years was a never-ending war waged by peaceful means; one young and deeply sensitive priest, drawing many thousands of people from all over Poland for his Masses for the Homeland, people otherwise afraid to speak up for their own rights, against a totalitarian state backed up by the military might of the Soviet Union. Paper copies and audio tapes of his sermons spread across the country. He did not urge his fellow Poles to take up arms. Truth was the sword he wielded. "An idea that needs rifles to survive will die of itself," he said.

Nor did he commit the modern error of separating the moral from the material. "The workers of August 1980," he said, "called more for moral order than for higher wages." Money can be printed. Prudence, temperance, courage, and justice cannot. Faith, hope, and charity cannot. The regime wanted to throw away a thousand years of Christian morality, and replace it with so-called secular morality, and that, for a Christian people, must ever remain a festering sore. Yet Father Jerzy did not recommend retreat into a secret chamber, for private devotion, while the world went on as it would. "There is no love without justice," he said, and love in turn finds strength in justice.

Love—not hatred. Violence may appear to triumph for a time, said Father Jerzy, but we who stand beneath the Cross know that love shall win the day.

Terrible as an army with banners

During this time, the communist government did not rest. Lies must sweat to retain the *status quo:* and let Catholics who are tempted to bow to the lies of our time take heed. Father Jerzy was under constant surveillance. The communists worked hard to turn the Polish hierarchy against him. They planted arms and explosives in his room to accuse him of treason. Pope John Paul, who supported Father Jerzy from the Vatican, said that the bishops of Poland had better stand up for him, or else *they* soon would find rifles under their beds too.

They tried to kill him by ringing his doorbell and throwing a bomb through his window. They tried to kill him by staging an auto accident. Thirteen times in 1984—in 1984, of all years—the secret police dragged him off for interrogation, while his supporters outside sang hymns and prayed. Meanwhile, the Soviets demanded that Jaruszelski shut the priest's mouth.

That the Polish communists did—to their loss in this world, and God knows to what shame in the next. On October 19, 1984, Father Jerzy and his driver were waylaid by three secret agents. The driver managed to escape and warn the Church, but the agents beat the priest with clubs, bound and gagged him, and threw him in the trunk. They smashed his skull. They crushed his teeth to the nubs. Finally, they loaded his unconscious body with a bag of rocks and cast him into a reservoir on the Vistula River. When divers found the body two weeks later, there were no legs, there was no face. Father Jerzy's brother identified him by a birthmark on his chest.

A million people attended his funeral. Men from Solidarity, square-jawed and grim, bore his coffin. "They wanted to kill hope," said Lech Wałęsa of the regime, "that it is possible in Poland to live without political violence," but the murder of the priest "exposes its deepest evil."

Father Jerzy overcame evil with love. He did not lash out against his tormentors. He urged his army of steelworkers to forgive, always. It was a power that American diplomats missed; to read their musings is like listening to a color-blind person talk about Fra Angelico. They thought that the Poles turned from communism to Solidarity without a violent upheaval just because Poles like to be orderly.

Perhaps they should have knelt beside the steelworkers at the Masses that Blessed Jerzy Popiełuszko said. Or prayed the litany to the Blessed Mother that he composed. One of the verses is simply this: "Mother of those who speak the truth, pray for us."

A Ring of Joy

Someone long after we are gone will have to explain why, with all our wealth and sophisticated machinery, our age has wrought so little in the arts to lift up the soul to wonder. Even a spiritual desert can rouse a man to seek the waters. Maybe we dwell in something worse than a desert.

Fra Angelico (c. 1395–1455) did not dwell in a desert. What the Catholic faith wrought in the arts in those days, and in his native Tuscany, is utterly marvelous. Painters whose names we may not even know, and painters of local repute in every little village, and such magnificent artists as Fra Angelico, colored the world with their happy visions. Some of these were sweet and earthy enough, as with the mischievous curly-headed urchins that make for angels by the hand of Fra Filippo Lippi, one of Fra Angelico's followers. But for Fra Angelico, the visions were heavenly, and of earth transformed by heaven.

A child in spirit

Guido di Pietro was born in the little village of Fiesole, atop the mountain overlooking Florence from the east. Like others, he learned his art when he was a boy, though we don't know much about his youth. Sometime in his twenties he joined the

Dominicans, and for them he did much of his work, beloved by his brothers for his gentleness and good humor.

Let me illustrate. It was said that Fra Angelico never took the brush unless he prayed first. For each of his brothers' cells at the convent of Saint Mark in Florence, he painted a fresco of a scene from the Gospel, and it was said that he could not paint the scene of the Passion without weeping. In 1446, Pope Eugene IV invited him to work in Rome, and while he was there the pope offered to make him Archbishop of Florence. Fra Angelico declined, saying that another friar was far worthier of the honor: the man we honor as Saint Antoninus. One time, Fra Angelico was invited to dinner by Pope Nicholas V, but when he came to the table he didn't know what to do, because he hadn't asked his prior for permission to eat meat. Apparently the pope's permission wasn't enough.

"He shunned the affairs of the world," says Giorgio Vasari, the great biographer of Italian artists, "and, living a pure and holy life, he was as much the friend of the poor as I believe his soul to be now the friend of heaven." He was sought after, and could command a high price for his work, but he never did. "You have real wealth," he said, "if you are content with little." He could have been an important man in temporal matters, but he said that obedience was less tiring, and you were a lot surer not to go astray. Great artists were celebrities in those days, but Fra Angelico said that the only dignity he sought was to avoid hell and draw near to heaven.

Fra Angelico wrote this epitaph for his tomb (I've translated the Latin):

Let it not be to my praise that I was
another Apelles,
But that I gave your riches, O Christ,
unto your own.
For the works of the earth are one thing,
the work of heaven another.
The city that bore me, John, is the Flower
of Tuscany.

The angel declared unto Mary

Cosimo de' Medici, the boss of Florence, rebuilt Saint Mark's at his own cost, and asked Fra Angelico to ornament it with paintings. I'll remark upon three of them here. The first is his famous *Annunciation.*

His brother Dominicans saw it as they walked up a flight of stairs, illuminated by light from a window out of view. It would be as if you could walk into another world, which is somehow our world too. Fra Angelico has cast the scene both indoors and outdoors. Mary is seated on a "throne" which is a mere wooden stool, as befitting her humility.

Her robe is a royal blue—a rich color, if you have to crush *lapis lazuli* to powder to make it. She is seated in a porch, its roof held up by Corinthian columns and gently pointed arches. We are to think of a palace, and of the Greek and Roman world into which the Church is about to be born.

Gabriel approaches her, dramatically, one of his wings partly hidden by a column. This is an *event*, happening in time and space. He leans forward in an attitude of honor, arms folded over his breast. Mary leans forward in the same posture. It's the moment when she says, *Fiat mihi*, and the Word is made flesh and dwells among us. How can that be, as she does not know man? There's a small window in the wall of the porch, between the angel and Mary. In it you can see reflected the nearby garden. But you might also think: just as light can pass through the glass of a window, the window remaining intact, so did the Holy Spirit make fruitful the womb of Mary, preserving her virginity.

To the left of Gabriel we see a garden stippled with white flowers, surrounded by a lowly wooden stockade fence, with nail-holes in each of the uprights. Why a garden? Fra Angelico is thinking of the verse from the Song of Songs, spoken by the bridegroom about the bride: *My beloved is a garden enclosed* (4:12), a garden of fragrant spices and fruit. We're meant to think of that other garden whence man was driven in punishment for his disobedience. A greater garden by far, a more glorious land of delight awaits us, because Mary has turned the key in the gate. Where that final garden is, we can guess from the colors in Gabriel's wings, the colors of the rainbow. He is a herald sent from heaven.

Every stroke is delicate and deliberate; deep peace pervades the whole. The painting is meant for wonder and prayer. At its base, Fra Angelico has painted two Latin verses, which I will translate:

When you pass by the figure of the Virgin
unbroken,
Take care lest you keep silent, and not cry out,
Hail!

Whiter than snow

The second is his *Harrowing of Hell.* Fra Angelico is the only painter I know who could paint white upon white, and make it seem as if the very robes were alive. The chief color in the scene is white, white against the plaster of Saint Mark's spare walls. Christ is robed in white, carrying his triumphant banner, a red cross on a white ground. All the accoutrements of hell are dull and trivial by comparison: the iron door at the Lord's feet, with a black devil squashed beneath it like an unpleasant bug; a couple of cowering demons to the left; and the dim mouth of the cave within.

But in front, in blessedness, what a scene! Jesus leans forward with a welcoming hand, as a very old man all in white, with long white hair and a white beard, races toward him—you can feel how eager he is! That is our ancient father Adam, the old man redeemed by the new Man, and sure enough he does resemble Jesus. Behind Adam rushes a crowd of souls, each graced as Adam is with a golden halo. We can see the faces of four. One is Eve, who looks like Mary in the *Annunciation*, with her hands crossed upon her breast. Another, whom Jesus called the "greatest born of woman," is the Baptist, shaggy and robust, his hands folded in prayer. Another is Aaron, robed as a priest. The fourth, to my eye, appears to be crowned. That would be David. And so we have Christ, priest and prophet and king, redeeming priest and prophet and king, and summing them all in himself.

Painting like a child

Now I come to his *Last Judgment*, a magnificent small altar piece, like a box of jewels. It's said that Fra Angelico first learned his trade by illuminating manuscripts, and sure enough, that care for the tiny detail is everywhere evident in his work. Here you see the saints in glory, their eyes raised to their Redeemer, or looking upon one another with joy and love. I know of no artist, not even Michelangelo, who seems to have felt so keenly that Jesus came to save *this man,* utterly unique, and *that woman*, utterly unique; no artist who knew as well as Fra Angelico that holiness makes us more distinct, more ourselves, and more fit for communion and friendship. You see a boyish soldier—George? A thoughtful queen—Margaret? A triple-tiara'd pope who cannot hold himself back—Gregory the Great? And, of course, Dominic, and Thomas Aquinas, and Catherine of Siena. They have to be there.

But what delights me most about this vision of glory is the scene to the left of the saints. It's another garden, with a palm tree growing up in the middle, and a circle of angels and children, dancing hand in hand. There was always something sweet and childlike about Fra Angelico and his art, and we recall the words of Christ, that if we want to enter the kingdom of heaven, we must become as little children. There's an old Italian song that is fitting here, which I'll render into English:

A garden blooms in heaven above
Where all the blessed, in a ring,
Their hearts aflame with holy love,
Return the love, and dance and sing.

So every saint a-caroling goes
With every angel in the reel,
Dancing before the heavenly Spouse
For love that they alone shall feel.

The Father of a Nation

"What are you doing, Medicine Man?"

The warrior, hardly more than a boy, sat cross-legged on the sand. He wore but a breech-cloth, and his strong arms and legs gleamed like bronze in the sun. The man he addressed was pale by comparison, though the many months outdoors had dried his face and hands to a leathery brown. He was a bit of a swayback. Just now he was leaning over the sand on the beach, tracing out strange lines and curls, lost in thought:

Consolavas benigno os bons pais que gemiam,
Restituindo às mães os filhos que perdiam.

"I'm making a song," said the man.

The boy knit his brows. Songs were wonderful things, like magic, like medicine. They could also be dangerous. "You are making a song to kill us!" he cried.

At that the man looked up and laughed. "No, Caua," he said, using the native Tupi language he had learned so well. "This is what it means. The mother is speaking to her son, who is God. She asks him to be kind, and to comfort the good mothers and fathers who weep, returning to them the children they have lost."

Losing children was a common enough thing. And worse. Caua knew an old woman who asked for her favorite tidbit while she lay dying: children's fingers. "Why do you make this song, Medicine Man?"

"To sing to the great Mother of God, Caua. And for you too."

"For us? Are we lost?"

"Not anymore," said the man, laughing.

On the road to São Paulo

The man, José de Anchieta, recalled the time when he first stood on the cliffs overlooking the Atlantic Ocean, cliffs that rise two or three thousand feet along the coast of Brazil. The place stank of dead fish drying in the summer sun, stranded there when the flooding River Tietê returned to its usual banks.

Dominus vobiscum, said the celebrant.

Et cum spiritu tuo, said José.

It was January 25, 1554, the feast of the Conversion of Saint Paul. There on the heights, set at some distance from the Portuguese colonists, he and twelve other Jesuits set up their first mission, their first college. Thus did they found the settlement of São Paulo, today the most populous city in the western hemisphere.

I'm looking at a painting of the event, by Antônio Parreiras. The priest faces a small congregation, just the other Jesuits and an old bearded

European. Anchieta stands nearest to us, reading from his missal. A long-haired native, stout and muscular, looks on with folded arms and one foot forward. Some naked natives in the distance seem to be approaching.

"José," the Jesuit provincial had said, "you are the best among us with languages." José nodded. It was true. He'd grown up on the Canary Islands, speaking Spanish, not Portuguese. He was a master at Latin, which he taught to the novices.

"You must teach us how to speak to these people." So he did.

Savages here and savages there

José Anchieta became the great apostle to Brazil, the father of the nation. Here some reader may cry, "But the Portuguese went there to establish colonies." True enough. That's the rule in human history. People see a bountiful land and they go there, especially if they believe they can use it in ways the natives cannot. Migrations have always meant war. Canaan was not empty when the children of Israel arrived.

What is *not* the rule in human history, what is inexplicable outside of the faith, is what José Anchieta and his fellow Jesuits did. He had not yet been ordained a priest, but he burned with the fire of the Good News. He wanted to save souls. To do that, he had to know the people as best he could.

He studied their ways, without contempt but also without sentimental indulgence, so that to this day his reports to his superiors in Portugal are invaluable works of anthropology. He compiled a dictionary and a grammar of the native Tupi language, so that Tupi and not Portuguese became the common tongue for communication between the Europeans and the various native tribes. He taught the natives how to work the land, so they would not be reduced to serfs on the Portuguese plantations. That often put him at odds with the Portuguese settlers, but so it was.

When we saw him scrawling poetry on the beach, it was because he had given himself as a hostage to the Tamoya, who were at war with the Portuguese and their allies among the Tupi. The Tamoya honored his courage. That was not wholly to his advantage, since it meant that, despite his lean and awkward form, they might kill and eat him to absorb that courage. They liked to fatten their human prisoners. Anchieta was a hostage long enough to compose, in his mind, a four-thousand-line poem in Portuguese, on dramatic moments in the life of the Blessed Virgin. He wrote the words in the sand as he composed them, to remember them when—or if—he would return to his brothers.

As for the cannibalism, the natives fed on man-flesh, said a Dutch explorer, not for hunger, but for inveterate hatred. "This day," he heard one warrior cry, "before sunset, your flesh shall be my roast meat!" Many of the Portuguese settlers believed that nothing could be done for a people so savage. But Anchieta and his fellow Jesuits took a dim view of the sins of the Portuguese, too, so that sometimes it seemed he was caught between savages on each side.

Still, it was a shock to him to see for the first time a cannibal feast, on Corpus Christi, of all days. The Tupi were glad to see him and made merry, eating and drinking and dancing, when one of them boasted that he had recently eaten a Portuguese slave, and called for one of his wives to fetch a leg he'd saved, to make a flute out of the shinbone. "You ate him," his friends laughed, "let us have some of him too!" So they sprinkled it with flour, said Anchieta, and gnawed away at it like dogs.

Eventually the Tamoya had to be defeated decisively in war, which Anchieta memorialized by the first epic poem written in the New World, his *De gestis Mendi de Saa*, on the accomplishments of Mem de Sá, the governor of Brazil. It is a remarkable work in sinewy Latin hexameters, indebted to Anchieta's vast reading in Virgil, Ovid, and Lucan, but quite original, and in part sympathetic to the people he had come to bring into the light.

For those works in Portuguese and Latin, José Anchieta is justly considered the father of Brazilian literature.

The play's the thing

Around the time that war ended, Anchieta was finally ordained a priest, and here we find him most busily at work. He had gifts both natural and supernatural. He had prophetic powers. He was sometimes surrounded by light, which he himself did not notice. He was a physician, and he taught the Tupi what he knew of the art of healing. He never rode a horse, but only walked, indefatigably, so that the path he wore from São Paulo to the principal settlement of the Portuguese at São Vicente, over forty miles away, was called Father José's Road. He could work for days without sleep. He attracted the natives by the gentle authority of his voice.

And by his playfulness, too. Pope Francis, who canonized Father José in 2014, said that the priest brought joy wherever he went. Joy is a fearful thing, said the pope. We must be brave to submit to it. Perhaps children are more apt to be taken prisoner by joy. Father José knew he should preach to the children before they fell into the savagery of their elders. He composed songs in Portuguese and Tupi, to delight them and teach them the stories of the Christian faith. He also wrote plays—think of the miracle plays of the medieval world, a vigorous and popular drama, on the lives of the saints or the Passion of Christ or the sorrows and joys of Mary. You mustn't imagine a formal stage and professional actors. Rather: bright costumes, natives in body paint, natives rattling the maracas, children kneeling roundabout the churchyard, torches, much song in both languages, and joy—the bright and mighty joy of the Gospel, victorious over the darkness of man's ancient enemy the devil. Father José did not want the children to grow up to be like their parents. He wanted the parents to grow into a spiritual childhood they had never known.

If you go to São Paulo, you can catch a play at the Father José Anchieta Theater. I do not know whether it will lift up your soul. But Father José is considered also the first great playwright of Brazil.

Saint José Anchieta died on June 9, 1597, in retirement at the seashore village of Reritiba, now called Anchieta in his honor. He is said to have converted over a million natives. I think he would have walked a thousand miles to baptize a single one.

The Seeker of Harmony

"Gather round, lads," says the friar, stooping over an odd contraption, with a string fastened at one end, while the other end, laid over a wheel, is fastened to a freestanding weight. In between are two frets, setting the length of the string to be plucked to make a musical note.

He plucks the string. "D," says one of the boys. They are dressed in the robes of novices. This is a house of the Minims, the severe and simple order founded by Saint Francis of Paola.

"Absolute pitch!" the friar laughs. It's impossible not to like him. He is blessed with a temperament that delights in everyone he meets—except for deists and pantheists, those pests. Skeptics he can work with.

"Now what happens if I move the frets closer, to shorten the string by half? Do you know?"

"Yes, Père Marin," says another novice, a mathematical amateur. "It will be D again, but an octave higher." The friar plucks the string, and the boys sing out D in falsetto, laughing. "Pythagoras knew that," says the priest. "But what happens if we move the frets back where they were, but double the weight that stretches the string? What do you think, boys?"

They volunteer various guesses, some saying that the note should be an octave higher, others a third or a fourth, until the priest stops them. "Lads, lads," he says, "you can't determine the answer by thinking about it. The Lord made the world as he made it, freely, and we must learn from it. We must not dictate to him how it should go. So we do the test."

He plucks the string.

"*Diabolus!*" cries the human pitch-pipe.

"Precisely," says the friar. "G-sharp. You see, I need the *square* of the weight to effect the octave. Four times the weight, not twice. Now what happens," he goes on, "if I keep the tension and the length the same, but use a string four times as thick? The sound will be lower, eh? Think of guitars. How much lower?"

"We must do the test," say the boys.

"We must do the test," says the priest, Marin Mersenne, father of the science of acoustics. "Never try to think in a vacuum," he says. "The good Lord made the world in measure, number, and weight, for us to behold and study in gratitude. What sound will this string make in a vacuum? None at all. The air is all around us, like water, and when the string vibrates, it's like a stone you toss into a pond, and the ripples in the air reach your ear." At which the bells ring for Prime.

Universal harmony

Marin Mersenne (1588–1648) was always fascinated by what made for harmony, how sounds are caused and how we experience them. He's the first man I am aware of to study the human vocal cords, the epiglottis, and the oral cavity as a musical instrument. He asks and tries to answer hundreds of questions about music. What happens to the sound when we change the *material* of the thing that vibrates? Why do we find pleasing the movement from unison to the major third (C, for example, to E), but *not* the movement from the major third to unison (E to the C above it)? How can we tune a keyboard so that we will hear the notes in concord with one another, regardless of the key we play in? If you play the piano, you are in debt to Mersenne.

Mersenne knew that Plato and his followers believed that music, with its approach to the immaterial, could raise the mind of man to the contemplation of God. For all his scientific investigation into the physics of sound, Mersenne believed it too. "If everything in the world," he wrote, "serves to raise us by degrees to God, the dependence of light upon luminous bodies, and of sound upon air, does not stand on the lowest rung. For these things should remind us of how we depend upon God, because neither of them is its own cause or its own subject."

The harmony of truths found in Mersenne an energetic investigator. In those days, the Christian faith was attacked on one side by *deists,* who reduced God to the world he created, and on the other by *skeptics,* who said that man could affirm nothing with certainty. Mersenne wrote against both, in an enormous compendium on the first six chapters of Genesis. "Music bears its own creed," he says, "for is it not God, as from the inexhaustible ocean of his delight, who pours forth upon us this small pleasure?"

A fellowship of Christians and scientists

For Father Mersenne, to ask about the world was to give thanks to God. We can see such Christian humility in his tireless and selfless friendships with more than a hundred of the great thinkers and scientists of his time. René Descartes was a timid hypochondriac, but Mersenne encouraged him, introduced him to others, and posed questions to him to sharpen his thought and to keep him on the sunny side of the faith. Galileo was a difficult man, but Mersenne sought him out, defended his research among other churchmen, and collaborated with him on mathematical problems. The most important of these involved the *cycloid,* the shape that a point on a wheel traces as the wheel rolls forward. It is no idle curiosity. What's the shape of the incline that makes an object go forward the fastest, given the laws of gravity? It isn't a diagonal. It's the cycloid, upside down. Mersenne's work helped another of his correspondents, Christian Huygens, to invent the pendulum clock.

From 1633 on, an academy of scientists formed itself in Paris, centered upon the person and the energy of Marin Mersenne. His knowledge was encyclopedic. He knew more of physics than did any but the best. He knew more of mathematics than did any but the best; and so forth with other fields of knowledge. That allowed him, since he had not a trace of envy in him, to put people and their works together. Nowadays, if you want to know who is doing work on prime numbers, you search online. In those days, you asked Father Mersenne, and he would send you the books he had, or put you in touch with the men themselves.

The academy met on Thursdays, and Mersenne took the lead, suggesting questions to the others; and Mersenne's questions were often more fruitful than other people's answers. He too worked on all kinds of things. One of them was to find a prime number higher than any previously known. (A prime number has no factors but itself and 1; 7, 11, and 13 are prime, for example.) Mersenne suggested a series of what are called Mersenne Primes, of the form 2n–1, for some integer n > 0. He claimed that 2127–1 and 2257–1 were prime. He was wrong about the latter, but correct about the former, which was for a long time the largest prime known (the seven largest primes currently known are all Mersenne primes). The field remains a great one for number theorists, cryptographers, and programmers.

Scaling the heights

What little do many today know about the Church and the advancement of human knowledge! At best they concede that there were a few scientists who *happened to be* faithful believers, with even a few priests here and there. They do not know that the Church took the lead in every path of research into every field. She was the nerve center, as wonder before God and his creation was the inspiring breath.

We can see as much when Father Mersenne went to Italy in 1644 to meet the young prodigy Evangelista Torricelli. The latter, educated by the Jesuits, had been sent to Rome at age eighteen by his uncle, a Camaldolese monk, to study the sciences. Torricelli had performed an important experiment on the weight of air—a matter that Blaise Pascal, who would also be welcomed into Mersenne's circle, would settle. Why can you use suction to bring water to a height of thirty-two feet, but no higher? To answer the question, Torricelli invented the mercury barometer, and Mersenne and he conducted a famous experiment, taking the barometer up a high mountain and noting the difference in the air pressure at the top. If you live in Denver, you know the air is thin. It was the young Italian and the French friar who first proved that air pressure decreases at higher altitudes.

But the truest heights for the good Christian friar were always those of wonder and thanksgiving for the gifts of God: first that man made in God's image should exist at all, and then that this same man, fallen into sin, should be redeemed and made new. For man, wrote Mersenne, was "testimony to the infinite wisdom of God, a most perfect work, indeed the aim of the world, its center, the embracer of all," a true cosmos in miniature. "O blessed man," said he, meditating on what it meant for Adam to be made in the image of God, "whom mercy watches over, truth instructs, justice governs, and peace fosters!" Mersenne can hardly contain his joy, to think that God "has pursued me with such love, me a worm, me a nothing, and prepared this universe for me as if for an emperor!"

Is that not motive enough to seek out the secrets of the world around us?

Flower of Zeal

The year is 1615; the place is Callao, the port of Lima in Peru. Cannons are booming out in the bay. They are the cannons from that great army of merchants, the far-sailing Dutch, bitter rivals of the Spanish. The friars of the convent of Saint Dominic rush to take up arms, to put up what weak defense they can.

Why the Dutch? The Spanish king, Philip III, was a scion of the Habsburgs, who ruled in much of central and southern Europe, and who laid claim to the Netherlands, where lakes of Dutch and Spanish blood had sunk into the earth. These Dutch were followers of John Calvin. They aimed to ally with the Indians to flank the Spanish in Peru—their ships to the west, the Indians pouring down from the Andes to the east.

Suddenly a woman appears, her sleeves rolled up and her religious habit clipped at the feet. "Rosa, dear Rosa, what are you doing?" cries one of the friars. "Go back home! The soldiers are coming." But Rosa was like a lion. "Who will be left to protect the Blessed Sacrament?" she said. "I am going now to the altar, to fight and die for it, if God wills."

If you go to Lima, you can see a painting of Saint Rose surrounded by Spanish soldiers, as she raises above her head a glorious monstrance, the Sacrament within it—Christ himself, the source, the bond, and the aim of our love.

Breaking the bars of enmity

We say of someone caught in an impossible bind that he is trapped between the devil and the deep blue sea. Rosa was faced with something like that. The Indians, whom she loved with the passion of a missionary (she herself was a Creole, of mixed Spanish and Indian blood), were given to idolatry, the worship of images, of stocks and stones. The Calvinists wanted to smash the images, and some of the missionaries leaned that way too. But Rosa found herself at odds with both sides—yet she considered the image-smashers to be the worse of the two. For she loved the Indians.

"Father Pedro," she said, to the Dominican priest who would one day make her known to the world, "I wish I were a man."

"Rosa!" he laughed. "A lovely woman like you—why?"

It is said that when she was a little baby with the name of Isabel, her mother had once looked upon her in the cradle, and it seemed that her face had the appearance of a mystical rose. Years later, the bishop Toribio, himself a canonized saint and a man who had baptized half a million natives, was about to confer upon her the sacrament of Confirmation, when all at once the Spirit inspired him to call her Rosa; and that became her true name.

"If I were a man," she said, "I could go out and preach and convert the Indians." She thought about it a moment, and smiled. "Let's make a trade, Father. I'll give you half of whatever good works I do, if you'll give me half of the souls you convert by your preaching."

"A deal!" said Father Pedro.

She was not simply jesting. A year before her early death at age thirty-one, Rosa adopted a baby Indian boy to raise him up to be a missionary. Her zeal for the missions bore fruit in the energy she lent to others. For everyone in Lima knew that Rosa had raised her eyes to the snow-clad mountains, beyond which she saw so many millions of poor souls who had never encountered the love of Jesus. Their lands were the true mines of Potosi, and the true miners were they who sought to win those silver and golden souls. Rosa said that Christ had destined the Indians to become precious stones of a new Jerusalem, to help to reform and build a Church renewed and strong. She had seen it in a dream. It was one of many such dreams.

Suffering and the anchor of a nation

It is hard for us to imagine how important Rosa was to both the people of Peru and the Spanish crown. We tear down statues and shrines. The Catholics of

Peru built them up. You can find images of Santa Rosa bearing an anchor as big as she was. It was the anchor of hope, for both the individual soul and the whole Spanish colony.

Her life had been one of hope. Rosa had from her youth dedicated her virginity to Christ, whom she called her Spouse. She mortified her flesh, fasting three times a week, making free use of the whip and the hair shirt, and pressing upon her brows a silver crown of thorns. We may shudder at those things. But who can deny the sweetness of the fruit? Rosa said that the suffering she endured was a great gift she had begged from heaven, an earnest that she would not have to endure the pains of Purgatory.

"I confess that I am a great sinner," she said to Father Pedro, "and yet my confidence is great, and great is the goodness with which my Spouse favors me. It is impossible for him to cease to bless me, so it is impossible for me to cease to love him." Why, she said, "it would be easier to make me believe that he had turned me into a stone, than that he should ever part from me." Even if heaven and earth combined in one to declare the contrary, she would not believe it, but rather she would put all her trust in God, "not that I merit anything," she said, "but that he is always faithful to his promise."

The veneration of Santa Rosa helped to bind the Spanish soldiers in confidence. She was, one preacher said, "Sion in arms," and "the celestial Cid"—referring to the hero of the medieval Spanish epic, who fought against the Moors. She was the "star of our souls," the "captain" in the fight to bring all South America into the true faith, with holy Mary as the conqueror. Warriors of all people understand why someone would embrace hardship, privations, and the imminent danger of death. Santa Rosa understood it.

Conquering in charity

But Rosa had always had to fight. Her parents did not approve of her decision to remain a virgin. For many years they kept her shut up in their home, so that she could not enter the convent. Still she did not disobey them, nor did she leave off her devotion to Jesus, especially to the Holy Child. If you go to the convent of Saint Dominic in Lima, you can see an astonishing sculpture of Santa Rosa, as if sleeping upon her bed of death, with a muscular child Jesus embracing her from above, as if he were Cupid and she his beloved Psyche, to dwell in joy together forever.

For Rosa did simple and womanly things to support her often difficult family when they could not support themselves. She plied the needle, and her works were so well prized for their beauty and delicacy that she could feed the family with her earnings, while she cared also for the sick and the poor of Lima. In this way she resembled two of her good friends, alive and busy in Lima at the same time. Those were the saints Martin de Porres and John Macias. What bonds of charity bound them all!—Rosa, the Creole woman born in Lima; Martin, the illegitimate mestizo also born in Lima, barred from Holy Orders, yet a wonder-worker in the shadows; and John, the orphan and peasant boy born in Spain, who crossed the seas to live as a Dominican lay brother, laboring in charity and prayer and silence.

A Rose of sweet savor

Santa Rosa foretold the day of her death, and when that day approached she fell gravely ill. Her mother came to her bedside and began to weep, but Rosa said, "Mother, please, don't shed tears for me. Tears are precious, and you should shed them only for your sins."

Rosa was racked with pain, and in her suffering, which partook of the supernatural, she made herself one with Christ upon Calvary. "Where are you, my Lord, my wealth, my prize!" she whispered. "Why don't I see you?" But then she was at peace, and she said, "Lord, fulfill in me your most holy will." Her last words were these: "Jesus, Jesus, be with me." Her countenance, upon her death, was adorned in blood.

And her death brought many people to life again. This again is hard for us to imagine. Crowds came to look upon her body, and when they saw her, they cried out, burst into tears, and confessed their sins. "From cold ashes and dry bones," says one of her biographers, "this holy woman was the most effective of preachers, rocking the foundations of society, reforming the consciences of the kingdom and the morals and manners of the whole city."

When Pope Clement X canonized her in 1671, he wrote that she was a "rose of the sweetest savor to God, to the angels, and to men," "the first of the New World to be numbered in the roll of the saints," breaking forth in that part of the church that had dwelt in darkness, gleaming like the dawn, shining with a light "like the full moon in our days, and like the sun refulgent in eternity."

Lord, let your Church bloom with such flowers once more!

Know the Ways

At the National Prayer Breakfast in Washington in 1994, a gentle old nun from Albania, Mother Teresa, dared to say that "the greatest destroyer of peace today is abortion," because by it we reject Jesus who said, *If you receive a little child, you receive me.* The audience, uneasy at first, broke into loud and sustained applause; a few sat in stony silence.

In our time, the saintly must prove itself to the political, which often stops up its ears. In the time of Saint Hildegard of Bingen (1098–1179) it was often the other way around: the political had to prove itself to the saintly. Hildegard, a holy woman, was a powerful voice in Europe, highly influential and highly regarded. She was called "The Sibyl of the Rhine," a woman of prophetic vision, much sought after for wisdom regarding matters earthly and heavenly. Had Mother Teresa lived when Hildegard did, she too would have been sought by priests and princes, bishops and kings. It takes real temerity, or blank ignorance, to turn away from words sent by God.

All the world in an egg

Out of the mouths of babes, says the psalmist, the Lord has fashioned praise. So it was in the life of

Hildegard. When she was only eight, her parents placed her in a Benedictine convent, though she was frail, and her eyes were so bad that she couldn't learn right away to read and write. But she *saw things:* she had visions. She never thought highly of herself for these gifts. In fact, she thought at first that everybody had them. They continued all her life long. Only when she was forty years old and abbess of the convent did the voice of God command her to put the visions in writing, and, after seeking counsel from her spiritual advisor, she did so, submitting them to the approval of her bishop. The pope himself, Eugenius III, encouraged her to continue. Notice the obedience. The work is called *Sci Vias: Know the Ways.*

Pope Benedict XVI said that Hildegard was a great exemplar of "the feminine genius," a rich soil, I would say, made up of humility and receptiveness, and the ability to see the holy in the smallest living things. God gave her to see the whole universe as an egg, held in place by three rays coming forth from a ball of fire. That was a sign of the Son of God coming to earth as a man, making known to us the things of heaven, and giving us cause to praise him, "incarnate of the true Maiden when the angel proclaimed him," and Mary, "alive in soul and body, received him in faith and joy."

The visions are far more intricate than I can describe. Hildegard herself drew illuminations of some of them, and they are like medieval rose windows—wheels within wheels, ranks within ranks, as with her extraordinary vision of the heavenly hierarchies of angels as nine concentric circles of faces, divided into sections of three, surrounding a central circle of pure white. Pope Benedict said that the visions are like those of the Old Testament prophets—think of Ezekiel and the valley of the dry bones. They are powerfully suggestive, founded in imagery that is rich in allusion to God's revelation, while also appealing to the universal experience of mankind.

Hope and life are green

Part of that experience that was close to Hildegard's heart was the goodness of the natural world. She was a collector of herbs, noting their various powers for healing and using them for the sisters in her abbey, so that some people say that she was the originator of natural science in Germany. Certainly she was fascinated with all things alive and green: *greenness* is ever on her mind when she thinks of the grace of God and the fertility of Mary's womb. Here is an antiphon she wrote for her sisters to sing for the office for virgins:

O noblest of all living green,
Who send your root into the sun,
And in a calmness full of light

Shine in a wheel beyond the bounds
Of any excellence of earth:
The rings of ministers divine
Enclose you in their bright embrace.
Like the first rose of dawn you blush,
Like the flame of the sun you burn.

Holy virgins above all, she seems to say, are green and fruitful. So in a letter to Saint Bernard of Clairvaux, she appeals to the Father who "through the sweet power of green vigor" sent the Word into the womb of Mary, where it became like "honey in the honeycomb." In another of her antiphons, she and her sisters beg the Lord to preserve them in their virginity, through the power of his love. Her language is bold indeed:

In the gift of your blood
We are wedded to you:
We who will know no man
Choose you, the Son of God.

Hammer of heretics

Hildegard was all the bolder because she submitted her mind and heart to the Church, and so she was trusted when the heresies of the time lifted their dark heads. These both had to do with the created world, and the Church's relationship to it. The Cathari—the "pure"—were like the Manicheans in the time of Augustine, believing that the physical world was fundamentally bad. The most ardent among them sought salvation by starving themselves, while the less ardent engaged in sexual sins with an easy conscience, since things of the body were not ultimately important. The followers of Arnold of Brescia, meanwhile, were stoked to fury over the wealth and ease of many churchmen, and Arnold finally declared that it was wrong for the Church to own any property at all.

People appealed to Hildegard, not for her to declare her opinion, but to ask her to pray that God might give her visions to help them find the truth. Here she writes to Pope Eugenius, on the firebrand Arnold: "He who is not silent speaks," she begins, as the mouthpiece of God. There's a jewel on the path, and a bear sweeps it up in his paw to close it in his bosom, but suddenly an eagle swoops down and snatches the jewel from the bear, hiding it in his wings till he presents it to the king in his palace. Be like the eagle, she cries to Eugenius!

As for the Cathars, Hildegard herself left her abbey for the great city of Cologne, to correct them and their shameful deeds—which, she said in words that God revealed to her, are "most vile in my sight." The created order itself was at stake, and the good of marriage, which is the work of the indivisible God.

The music of the heavens

But I should like to conclude with something true and beautiful. Hildegard, who never had a formal education, is the medieval composer from whom we have the greatest number of works, for which she usually wrote both the texts and the music. The songs are sung in unison, as is the rule for Gregorian chant. But Hildegard set the melodies specifically for the words. If you know what the words mean, she seems to say, you will know why you are singing those notes and not others. Most especially you will let your heart be raised by the long and soaring melismas, plays upon a single syllable. The opening "O" of *O nobilissima viriditas* lingers over twenty-two notes; the second syllable of the word *divinorum* plays lovingly over fifty-nine notes. Imagine her convent of women, with their sweet female voices, raising her haunting strains of sound in praise of the eternal Bridegroom.

"You are taken up into heavenly places," said the scholar and abbot Odo of Soissons, who marked it as a sign of God's favor that though Hildegard had never studied music, she could compose so marvelously. She too thought of it as a gift and not as her own production. The title of her book of music says as much: *Symphonia harmoniae caelestium revelationum,* "The symphony of the harmony of heavenly revelations." If Adam had never fallen, his voice, said Hildegard, which God had made to resound with the harmonies of every created thing, would have been too wonderful for our weak human nature to endure.

Saint Hildegard has become popular among some in our time, but for the wrong reasons, just as many people admired or pretended to admire Mother Teresa, while ignoring what she was all about. Hildegard made her music, I should say, because she *listened.* And that is what obedience is all about.

The Grave of the Unknown Missionary

Sometimes things are too close to us to see, or too common to notice: the blue of the sky, to which no flower or bird's wing can compare; the different beauties of man and woman, which we take for granted and often mar; the piping of a child's voice, which through all the changes of his life will remain that same voice, colored and deepened but the same.

So with the gifts of grace. We forget how extraordinary they are, dramatic, world-changing, incomprehensible outside of the Church. Not one of us would be in the Church at all were it not for the *missionary*, one *who has been sent*, fulfilling the Lord's great commission, to *make disciples of all nations, baptizing them in the name of the Father and of the Son and of the Holy Spirit*. Said Saint Paul, the Apostle to the Romans: *But how can they call on him in whom they have not believed? And how can they believe in him of whom they have not heard? And how can they hear without someone to preach? And how can people preach unless they are sent?* Paul was sent, but not with letters of safe conduct. *Five times*, he says to the Corinthians, *I have received at the hands of the Jews forty lashes minus one. Three times I was beaten with rods, once I was stoned, three times I was shipwrecked, I passed a night and a day on the deep; on frequent journeys, in dangers from rivers, dangers from robbers, dangers from my own race, dangers from Gentiles,* and more. His life of preaching makes the life of a soldier of fortune look like a tea party at home.

The sagas of the saints

Odysseus spent ten years besieging Troy and sacking it when it fell; then he spent ten years trying to sail back to Ithaca. Aeneas brought his people from Troy after it had fallen, and then wandered about the Mediterranean before he settled them upon the Italian shores, not without war, where their descendants would establish Rome and her empire, not without war. The tales have power to stir our hearts still. So do the sagas of the pagan Germans, sagas of courage, cunning, vengeance, treachery, and loyalty to one's lord when all is lost. These are all tales of a ruined king, man, still bearing some traces of his royalty, so that we can admire him as he fights his way to one doom or another, to dark perdition or to sometimes darker victory.

In no pagan society, ancient or modern, is there anything like the saga of the missionary. The young Joseph de Veuster stows himself aboard a ship to Hawaii so that he can minister to pagan lepers on Molokai. When he arrives he finds unspeakable moral and physical squalor, and he is in no way welcome. He himself will die of leprosy, eventually. Had he died or been murdered in his first year in Hawaii, we would not know his name, and his bones might have been picked apart by the fishes in the sea.

The bishop Boniface goes to the woods of Germany, to preach to the warlike pagan tribes. He will be martyred, but not before he plants the cross of Christ as the true Yggdrasil, the only Tree of Life. Boniface did not go alone. Who were the priests who accompanied him? We do not know them all, we do not know the suffering they endured, we do not know where their bones rest.

Francis Xavier goes to the east with his fellow Jesuits, sowing the seed of faith among the Japanese. That stirring tale seemed to come to a dead halt when the ruler Hideyoshi tried to eradicate Christianity from his realm, murdering those, like Saint Paul Miki, who refused to deny Christ. These are the sweet and delicate pink blooms of the flowering plum, but how many hundreds of priests and nuns and Christian laymen whose names we do not know are the roots, the pith, the sap, and the bark of that tree? We will know their sagas in that city above where no stories are lost.

What moves the soul?

When Julius Caesar went to Gaul, he left a trail of genocide, and Roman outposts that would become the towns of France. He did it to attain the glory he needed to win preeminence over his rivals in Rome, writing about his campaigns with a sangfroid that doesn't surprise us, because it is the sort of thing that warriors and statesmen do. When the English came to Virginia, they found tribes of natives in inveterate war against each other. That doesn't surprise us. It is what tribes do. Peoples migrate at the edge of a sword.

But what moves the missionary? Frances Cabrini was frail of body, but she went to Pope Leo XIII to ask permission to go with her sisters to China. He told her to minister to the Italian immigrants in the United States instead, but what could have moved Mother Cabrini to want to do so dangerous a thing? What made Matteo Ricci study Chinese for many years before he himself, utterly vulnerable, went to that old and mysterious China, finding his way into the Forbidden City itself? Not hunger for riches or land, but hunger for souls—the love of souls.

It's hard to explain to the world, this love. The world knows avarice and ambition, but nothing like the missionary's love. Imagine—you are a French boy living in Algiers after a cholera epidemic, and your archbishop, the great Cardinal Lavigerie, says that the orphans need to be taught, and would you like to join his new Missionaries of Africa? He has more in mind, too. Your eyes widen as he tells you of his further intent, to go bring the Good News to the Arab Muslims and to the pagans of central Africa.

Why would you do it? It means poverty, hard labor, suspicion, persecution; the feverish jungles of the Congo; the vast hot sands of the Sahara. Three of your fellows are murdered on their way to the great desert trading post of Timbuktu. Why not just sing to the Lord in Algiers, under French rule, and let God sort out what he will do with pagans and Muslims? If God loves them, let him decide.

But God has chosen to save men by men. "Be fruitful and multiply," he commands us from the beginning, to fill the earth and subdue it by love. How will people know that God loves them unless we whom God has sent love them?

An army beyond counting

Let us honor, then, those foot-soldiers of the faith, the uncounted hosts of missionaries whom God has sent, moved by an otherwise inconceivable love.

Before there was ever a secular organization drawing on the moral capital of the Christian faith to bring food to the hungry, there were missionaries, bringing the olive and the grape to Californian natives who had been reduced by stronger neighbors to eating lizards. How many bowls of rice and soup have been prepared by the hands of an unknown missionary, who might have been living in unobjectionable comfort back at home? How many loaves of bread did they bake, and how many ovens did they build to bake the bread? How many fields sown with grain? How many orchards and vineyards? With what short fare did they feed their lean forms, so that others, even those who were wary of them and might kill them, could feed? Before there were doctors without borders, there were missionaries without borders, to bring medicine to the sick, and sometimes ruining their own health to do it. What hospitals did the Romans establish in the nations they overcame? None, for the hospital itself is an invention of the Church. The Samaritan happened upon a man who had fallen among thieves, left for dead by the wayside. But the missionary actively *seeks out* those who have been left for dead. How many men and women of the Church have gone among the sick, to pour oil and wine into their wounds and bind them up? Mother Teresa cared for those in Calcutta whom the most religious of the Hindus would not touch. She lived with them. She broke bread with them. She cleaned their bodies with her own hands. But she had become only the most visible face of her order, and now thousands of women all over the world do those humble things, what the world does not see.

Who has taught the ignorant? Wherever the missionaries went, they brought writing and reading to those who had none. The first written works in many a human language have been accomplished by missionaries, who often had to invent or adapt an alphabet to do so. How far that is from the conqueror who is pleased to keep his conquered peoples in darkness! Imagine a patient man in a black robe, a patient woman in the habit of a nun, guiding the finger of a child as he traces out the first mysterious character of knowledge. Multiply it by millions.

Then the most important of all, the faith. Those who have it know that nothing is greater. Imagine the light breaking upon a human soul. Missionaries are bearers of that light. We cannot know here to how many we ourselves are indebted. But in the kingdom of God, I think there will be many a time when we will say, "Ah, then, that was you!" For there is nothing hidden that shall not be brought to light.

He Trains My Fingers for Peace

"Little War-god," said the servant, resting after the long march, "why are you scrubbing my boots?"

The boy looked up and smiled. He was a strapping lad of fifteen, tall, with muscles like cords from the military life he had always known. "The Lord I serve once washed the feet of his disciples, and told them they should go and do the same," he said.

"The Lord you serve," said the servant, considering. The emperor Constantine served that Lord. So did many of the soldiers. It was strange. A soldier's life was rough. It wasn't just the bloodshed, another man's very life staining your hands. There was the filth of pitching camp, digging trenches in a square, and throwing up the earth as bulwarks; the hard fare, often wrested from farms they passed through; women hanging about the camps, trading favors for favors; rough talk, superstitions; but this boy was pure. Even the old pagan veterans loved him. So did the servant.

"I remember when you first went to the church, Little War-god," he said. "Your father was in a rage all day. I have the scars on my back to show it."

Martin set down the boots and lighted a fire for their meal. "I know," he said. "I pray for my father, just as I pray for you." They ate together, as always.

"He couldn't say it wasn't Roman," said the servant, thinking of the emperor.

"It will be more Roman than Rome," said the boy.

The beggar on the road

Ambianum—we call it Amiens—wasn't as frigid as the Alps in the winter, but it could be more miserable, with its snow and slush and long cold rains. This winter was especially bad, and many did not survive it.

The young Martin had been sent to this place in northern Gaul with his regiment. That was no surprise. Constantine had come from Britain, the empire's frontier in the northwest. Rome had fallen into the middle of nowhere, as far as governing was concerned. The emperor was in his new city in the east. It was the soldier's lot to shore up the thousands of miles of frontier open to invaders. And there were enemies from within, too, as Martin was aware.

He was riding out of the city, wearing only his armor and his soldier's cloak, when he met a naked beggar at the gates, crying out to all who passed by. They were cold too, so they looked the other way.

"Have mercy on me, young master," said the beggar.

Martin pulled his horse to a halt. He took his cloak and his sword, and he did what probably no

Roman soldier had ever done. He cut the cloak in two and gave half of it to the beggar. The other half he draped about himself. It did not cover him.

"Little War-god," some of his fellows laughed, "we should call you Cupid now, the naked boy!"

But others looked on and sighed. They had more to clothe the beggar with, but they did not do what Martin did.

That night Martin fell into a deep sleep, and in a dream he saw Christ surrounded by an army of angels. "Martin, a catechumen until now, has clothed me in this robe," said the Lord, recalling his words that what we do for the least of these his little brothers, that we do for him.

Martin then knew that he would lead a life of apostolic poverty. A few years later he left the army and traveled to Milan to see his parents one last time. On the way the devil confronted him, saying, "Wherever you go and whatever you try to do, I will fight against you!" But Martin replied with the psalmist, "God is my help; what shall I fear that man can do to me?" And the devil vanished.

On the road

Martin then went to Poitiers to become a disciple of the great bishop Saint Hilary. Those were years of terrible controversy in the Church, when the faith was locked in mortal combat with the Arian heresy. Had the Arians triumphed, the Church would have degenerated into a unitarian benevolent society, doomed to wither and die. There's all the difference in the world between believing that God sent a man named Jesus to speak in his name, and then "adopted" him as first of all creatures, and that God himself became man to save man. *That* was God battering down the walls of a sinful world, to build it new again.

Hilary was a tireless fighter for the orthodox faith. But some opposed him and drove him into exile. At that, Martin withdrew into the solitude he had longed for, on the island of Gallinaria, off the Ligurian coast. But that was just the beginning. Martin's life is a drama of self-giving, from the desert-dweller—that is what *hermit* means—to the solitary—that is what *monk* means—to the humble overseer—that is what *bishop* means. He was made strong by the military drill—that is what *ascetic* means—of the Christian soldier. When Hilary was given leave to return to Poitiers, Martin joined him, and in a solitary plain several miles away he and his fellows built a monastery, each monk dwelling in his own cell.

But military drill is for military action. Many a road of the Roman Empire, laid down by soldiers, has lasted these two thousand years. Martin often left his cell to hit those roads, preaching the faith in central and western Gaul. He was so beloved as a preacher and a wonder-worker that when the bishop of Tours died in 371, the priests cried out for Martin to take his place.

That wasn't easy. Martin was devoted to his solitary life. "Martinus," cried the man on his knees, begging, "my wife is near death. Please come and lay your hands upon her!" For Martin had once raised a dead man to life, a slave who had hanged himself. Martin drove the crowd of mourners away, and he lay upon the body and prayed, whence life returned to the man. So Martin set forth on the road to Tours. But suddenly he saw great throngs of people, not just from Tours but from all the towns around, to lead him into the city—that is, to keep him from getting away. There had been no sick wife. It was a ruse to make Martin bishop.

The last shall be first

"This, for a bishop?" cried the more worldly and ambitious men of the clergy. "Look at his face, his filthy clothes, his shaggy hair!" But others said that those men were quite mad, as Martin was a mighty defender of the faith. The common people agreed. The controversy was settled in a striking way. The regular lector couldn't get through because of the crowds, so someone was chosen at random to come up and read the first passage his eyes might light upon as he opened the scriptures.

Out of the mouths of babes and sucklings you have fashioned praise, he read from the eighth psalm, *on account of your enemies.* Martin's election followed forthwith, on July 4.

He did not give up his simple ways. He wore a shirt of camel's hair, nothing softer. He retired to a cell sometimes to be in solitary prayer. Others gathered round him, and they established the monastery of Marmoutier. He was filled with zeal for the truth, preaching tirelessly, attracting souls by his humble life and his uncompromising and stalwart orthodoxy. It must have been a sacrifice for him to travel so much, but that is what he did, both to battle the heretics and to protect them against fiery bishops and statesmen who wanted to put their leaders to death. In this regard he was like Saint Ambrose, who threatened the emperor Theodosius with excommunication unless he repented of his massacre of civilians at Thessalonica.

Martin of Tours was one of the best-loved saints whom God has given to the Church. Many were the miracles he performed, and great was his devotion to the poor. He helped to make Gaul firm in the faith—or, we may say, his sowing the seeds of truth would one day come to blossom in the nation called France. He died on November 8, three days before his feast day.

War and peace

I will end with two more scenes. It is 1793. The revolutionists, heeding the call of the ingrate Voltaire to "tear down the infamous thing," have smashed the church in Tours that housed the bones of Saint Martin. They leave standing two towers, but lay down roads on either side so that the basilica might never be built again. They did not get their way entirely. The atheistic furor passed, and Martin's tomb was dug out many years later, and a new basilica was built to house them.

It is early morning on the Feast of Saint Martin, 1918. Marshal Ferdinand Foch and his aide stand outside a railway car in the forest of Compiègne. Near him is the British legate, and representatives of Germany and Austria-Hungary. They have signed an armistice ending World War One. It will go into effect, by Foch's order, at 11 AM, the eleventh hour of the eleventh day of the eleventh month. Foch, whose brother was a priest, had in mind Saint Martin, that soldier for peace.

The Rock of Ages

The year is 1684. Imagine a couple of rich merchants, well stuffed from a good dinner, walking the streets of Hamburg, the great mercantile city on the River Elbe.

"The bishop is a fool or a hypocrite or both. No man can live the way he does."

"They say he has only bread and beer four days a week."

"It's gone to his brain."

"He studies the brain, doesn't he?"

"A heretic. Why would he sell his bishop's ring? Why doesn't he wear the robes of his office? Giving all to the poor, indeed!"

"Regard the lilies of the field, how they grow."

"Don't talk to me about lilies. We must get rid of this pest. The people of Hamburg know that God rewards the pious. He is an anatomist, yes? Let's give him some of his own to study."

"What do you mean?"

"Cut off his ears and nose."

A man of careful observation

The bishop, Nicolas Steno (1638–1686)—Niels Steensen, as he was christened in his native Denmark—had grown up as a frail little boy in a devoutly Lutheran home. He couldn't play with the other children, so instead he learned to listen to the grownups and their talk about serious matters. He became a man of many learned friends, with the patience to look at things very closely before pronouncing upon them.

By the time he was thirty, Steno had made a whole lifetime of discovery in several fields of science. His first love was anatomy. He discovered the tube that brings saliva from the gland to the mouth; it is called *Stensen's duct.* He said, against common opinion, that when muscles contract, their shape changes but not their volume. The ancient physician Galen had said that the heart was the fireplace of the body, and most scientists agreed, but Steno, anticipating the anatomist William Harvey, described the heart as a double pump. He also said, correctly, that the body's cells are nourished by contact with all manner of fluids, not only by the blood in the tiniest capillaries.

His *Discourse on the Anatomy of the Brain* is the first of its kind, treating of the folds and fibers and the different organs within the organ. "I must confess that I know nothing about it," he says in his introduction. He was humble enough to admit it, and brave enough to rebuke famous men who claimed to know more than they did, such as his friend Descartes, who said that the human soul resided in the pineal gland. They "will give you the history of the brain and the disposition of its parts as assuredly as if they had been present at the fashioning of that magnificent organ, and had penetrated into all the designs of its great Architect." It was, he said with deep wonder, "the most beautiful masterwork of Nature."

Stone within stone

In 1666, we find him in Italy, teaching at the University of Padua, where Harvey himself had studied, and where Vesalius, the founder of modern anatomy, had taught. He was an intellectual star. So when a couple of fishermen caught a huge shark off the Ligurian coast, the Grand Duke of Tuscany, Ferdinand II de' Medici, ordered that the head be sent immediately to his friend, Steno.

The triangular teeth interested him most. People had noticed odd triangular "stones" locked inside other stones, far from the sea. What were they, and where did they come from? Some said they were produced internally, by power inherent in the rock. Others said they were formed by the force of the sun or the moon. But Steno knew that the material was organic, not like inorganic rock: think of chalk or limestone, composed of the stuff of bones and shells. They must be the petrified remains of real teeth—which meant that the hills where they were found must once have been underwater. Steno, a devout Christian, thought straightaway of Noah's flood.

That led him to ask a tricky question: How can a solid end up wholly encased within another solid? How do we get stones inside stones? How do we get veins of metal between fissures of rock? What about crusts of crystals and gems? The principles he came up with are not obvious. They involve the gradual turning of fluid stuff to solid. Say you have a stone with an impression upon its surface—what we now call a fossil. Steno said that the object that made the impression came before, or had been hardened before, the rock upon which it made its mark. New Hampshire, where I live, is full of conglomerate rocks, heavy things that seem made of hardened mud, studded with chunks of quartz and other crystals. Steno's Law says that the crystals came first.

But what if you find copper running through layers of basalt, as they did in Italy? Then, said Steno, it was the basalt that came first, and the copper later. If you think of volcanic pumice, you will see how rock can, under great pressure and heat, be opened up with pores and veins into which liquid metal can flow. For all rock, he said, had once been fluid, and fluid settles evenly and horizontally, according to its weight. Suppose you are driving along a road cut through the granite of a hillside, and you notice strips of color in the rock, strips that are not parallel to the horizon. They must once have been parallel, Steno said, but now they are tilted because of *subsequent* events: think of the pressure of a slow collision, or, he said, of "the spontaneous slipping or downfall of the upper strata after they have begun to form cracks"—what we now call *faults.*

What about those crystals? Steno surmised that they did not grow from within, like organisms, but from without, by accretion—think of coral. He did not know about electrical charges, but he guessed that some inner force, something like magnetism, made it so that a crystal of a certain material, regardless of its size, would always have *the same angles between its faces.* Think of the hexagons of a snowflake.

Nicolas Steno is justly considered the father of paleontology, and of the study of geological strata. His work was far ahead of its time.

Substance beneath accident

"You're not afraid of the truth, young Nicolas," said the gentlewoman. "You must go where the truth leads." It was early summer in the port city of Livorno, under the jurisdiction of Ferdinand II de' Medici, the young scientist's friend and patron. People of all faiths lived and traded in Livorno. But today, a Thursday, Corpus Christi, was a holiday for the Catholics, and the great piazza in front of the Cathedral of Saint Francis was thronged with the faithful. The bishop came forth bearing the monstrance, followed by a long train of priests and altar boys, as the choir chanted from the hymn of Thomas Aquinas:

Praestet fides supplementum
sensuum defectui.

"I do not see the Body of Christ," said the scientist.

"Not with the eyes," said she, the good and pious lady of Lucca. "That's true. It's the mind that sees, not the eyes."

The procession came their way. Signora Arnolfini fell to her knees. So did Nicolas Steno, humbly. "I'm not sure," he said.

"Then you must study. Read the Fathers. Promise me," she said, smiling, but with urgency. "Promise me that. Ferdinand wishes the same."

"I promise."

The young man kept his word. He read his way into believing that Christ was truly present in the Eucharist, Body, Blood, soul, and divinity, under the appearances of bread. How can it be? Who can penetrate a miracle? Perhaps he was thinking of that too, along with all the other works of God that he had studied, when he said, "Fair are the things we see, and fairer are the things we know. But fairest of all are the things we do not know."

On All Souls' Day in 1667, Steno entered the Catholic Church. He had long been a student of theology, and he continued in that work, even as he was engaging in his scientific investigations. In 1675, he was ordained a priest, in Florence, and celebrated his first Mass, fittingly enough at the Basilica of the Most Holy Lady of the Annunciation—of that moment when divinity was enclosed within the matter of the womb of Mary.

A pilgrim and preacher to the end

Steno's scientific work had taken him far afield. So would his priestly work. Pope Innocent XI sent him back north to German lands, as the Vicar Apostolic for the Nordic Missions, a newly created vicariate that would last until 1930. He went to Hanover and then to Hamburg, where he was an auxiliary bishop. Those were wealthy cities, and the people made fun of him for his life of poverty and self-denial. They even threatened to mutilate the one-time anatomist. Worldly people do not like to be shown up.

Blessed Nicolas Steno died, exhausted, in 1686. His bones rest in the Basilica of Saint Lawrence, in Florence, where he had known his happiest days. Would that we were all as devoted to the truth as he was.